GO BACKPACKING!

GO BACKPACKING!

MATT STONE

PRUETT

PRUETT PUBLISHING COMPANY
BOULDER, COLORADO

Printed in the United States of America

11 10 09 08 07 06 05 04 03 02   5 4 3 2 1

Library of Congress Cataloging-in-Publication Data

  Stone, Matt, 1978–
  Go backpacking! / by Matt Stone.
     p. cm.
  ISBN 0-87108-926-2 (alk. paper)
  1. Backpacking. 2. Stone, Matt, 1978—Travel. I. Title.
  GV199.6.S84 2005
  796.51—dc22
                          2005014007

Illustrations by Jessica Bella Dodds
Design by MacWorks

CONTENTS

INTRODUCTION

Backpacking, as you may already know, is one of the most wholesome and fulfilling hobbies a human being can have. The exercise is good for the body, being outdoors away from your troubles is good for the mind, and seeing nature without as much human interference, feeling like you're actually a part of it, is nothing short of spiritual. Through my backpacking I've encountered coldness, wetness, tiredness, headaches, blisters, bug bites, even leeches, but it's the discomforts that make backpacking the amazing thing that it is. The idea of backpacking itself sounds like a strenuous ordeal, a lot of trouble for a small reward, but it's not. Backpacking will probably always be something that only a small percent of humans do, which is a good thing to keep primitive areas from getting destroyed; however, the enjoyment I've had over the years is something I'd wish upon anyone.

I started backpacking not too terribly long ago. It all began with a father-and-son trip that you will hear much about in this book. I didn't grow up in a gung ho backpacking family. In fact, it was my dad's first trip too. It was certainly a crash course, but learning the hard way is the most effective way to learn, and that's exactly what I've had to do. It always amazes me that the stupid and painful mistakes that I make don't keep me from having the best times of my life. Spending long sleepless nights with a big rock nudging me in the back or getting attacked by mosquitoes or having sores on my hips from a poorly fitting backpack aren't the first memories that pop into my head. The things I remember are seeing a mountain goat for the first time, standing on top of a 13,000-foot peak, feeling the peace and rejuvenation of being completely alone for four straight days.

Although you will forget most of your discomforts, it is important to reduce those discomforts as much as possible. If your first trip is a huge ordeal, your second trip may not come for a long, long time. During my first three years of backpacking, I think I went, hmmm, about three times. Now I try to get out at least a couple of times a month. Spending 30 or 40 nights out a year is becoming a regular pattern, but I admit, 30 or 40 nights doing it like I did my first few years would have been pretty rough. Carrying obscene amounts of stuff in a pack that didn't fit, spending hours getting ready for the trip and still not really knowing if I was actually prepared, and eating a combination of bland and unhealthy food made frequent backpacking unwanted and impractical. You start to feel like it's not worth all the trouble, and that's what I wish to help you avoid. It can be easy and painless, I promise. I'm not the almighty guru of backpacking rights and wrongs, but I do hope to get you thinking about things a little differently and point you in the right direction.

The good news is that making it easier and more enjoyable isn't hard. It was tough trying to figure it all out on my own, especially as an 18-year-old, but I'll take you through several shortcuts that took me several long, wet, cold, blistered years to discover. Hopefully you won't have to carry a 60-pound pack for a three-day trip that's full of potatoes, enough candle lanterns to open up a church, and more clothes than you even knew you owned. Hopefully you won't have to go through three rooms and two closets to find your gear before a trip. Hopefully you won't forget the small things like a lighter, eating utensils, and toilet paper. I can now pack for a trip in 10 minutes, remember everything, and fit it all in a daypack if it's a one-nighter. I even have my backpacking food organized and ready to go at a moment's notice.

Of course, the hardest thing about backpacking is organizing and planning for the first trip. Even more difficult to overcome is buying the equipment you need without spending thousands of dollars. If you've never been, you want to go, and you have nothing, well, it's going to cost you, but there are several ways to save money too. Don't be intimidated or turned off by the investment of time, energy, and money that it takes to get ready for your first trip. There are ways of making it easy and affordable, and you'll never regret it. It's just not possible.

Another thing that can discourage you from going that you must overcome is the "how and what to cook" thing. Cooking outside can be intimidating for beginners. If you find yourself looking at backpacking stoves and wondering how on earth you could ever cook anything decent and manage to keep from starting a forest fire in the process, then you are not alone. You can be taught! Although many stoves look like they are more difficult to operate than a space shuttle, they are all pretty easy to figure out. Even the most complicated ones only require a few pumps on a fuel bottle, a half turn of a knob, and a match to light. They're not any more difficult to operate than one uh them lean, mean, grillin', fat annihilatin', arteries-still-be-gettin'-clogged Foreman grills.

What to eat is even simpler. If you don't want it to be difficult, then there are plenty of things for you to cook that take five minutes and are packaged nicely in a single container. I'm talkin' mac 'n' cheese, baby. If you're a "do it all yourself from scratch" type of person, well, that's pretty easy too, but it does take a little cooking intuition and some practice. I highly recommend being a "do it yourself from scratch" person, but then again, I cook for a living so keep that in mind. Backcountry cooking is certainly a fun hobby if you get into it, though, and a homemade meal made in the wilderness can only add to your experience.

Backpacking is simply too good of a hobby to miss out on. It never gets repetitive unless you let it. There are millions of acres of wilderness in the United States alone to explore, enabling even the most ambitious hiker to see something new each trip for a lifetime. Backpacking is great outside of North America also. In the Himalayas, for example, much of the tourism is geared towards tourists coming into the country, wanting to see those massive, rugged mountains. Even in a country as remote and isolated as Nepal, organizing a trek is easier than you can ever imagine, and I highly recommend backpacking as a traveling activity. There's really no better way to really see and feel a foreign culture and landscape.

Another key to really enjoying it is doing it often. I've always enjoyed backpacking and hiking, but it wasn't until I began doing it regularly that I really started to become an addict. The more you do it the easier it gets, and pains and discomforts are replaced with peacefulness and joy. If you only go once a year you'll find yourself waking up in your tent the next morning and wondering if you aged 40 years overnight. Your legs and back are so stiff it's hard to get yourself out of your bag, much less stand up and hike another eight miles. I find that the best possible way to make backpacking more enjoyable is to simply do it every chance you get. You do have time, you do have the money, it doesn't matter what the weather is like, the Broncos will still win even if you're not there to watch, your world won't collapse if you can't check your voice mail for a couple of days.

My goal in this book is obviously to encourage you to go, and to go frequently. Yes, it sounds risky—more people running around in the woods ruining it for those in search of a little peace and quiet, but it's okay. There's nothing wrong with an increased number of people enjoying wilderness areas by foot, especially if they make a genuine effort to minimize their human impact. Maybe increased backpacking will even inspire a few more people to make sure that we'll always have plenty of places to go with our backpacks and boots. Would that be so bad?

You might have picked out this book because you've backpacked before, and it was so painful that you're seeking the help of a professional before making another attempt at it. You might have picked out this book because you've never been and want to get started, or you might have picked it out because you're an addict like me and just want to read about backpacking. In any case, you're reading the right book for you. Although much of the book is geared toward beginners, even someone who has been a thousand times can learn a few new tricks and maybe even enjoy reading this literary masterpiece that I have created.

Enjoy. I hope the poetic prose that follows sparks you to have many an outdoor adventure, helps solve a backpacking dilemma or two, and occasionally evokes a chuckle. But, if it's a nice sunny day, you've got the next couple of days off, and you're sitting around on your couch reading this, you're in so much trouble. I'd rather you use this to start a campfire (in a well-established fire ring surrounded by an abundant source of dead twigs and branches of course, and oh yes, remember to put it out). Please, for the forsaken love of all that is divinely holy: Go backpacking!

"Hey Dad,

did you see these?" I said holding up a small candle lantern, complete with plastic case and a hook on top for hanging.

"Oh those look pretty cool, I saw 'em earlier but I didn't know what they were."

"Yeah, they're candle lanterns. Look, you can push them together and they get even smaller."

Our excitement about this little gadget sounded sirens of profit in one of the salesmen. "Hi, can I help you fellas find anything? These are neat aren't they? They've got a hook on top too. I hook mine right inside my tent, and it's bright enough to read a book or play cards or whatever." Visions of a cozy warm tent and a game of cards ran through our minds.

"Uh, yeah, we're actually going backpacking for the first time," my dad said. "We've got rain jackets, boots, and one sleeping bag and that's about it." Being in the town's only outdoor store and making a comment like that made us the store owners' new best friends. Not only was our salesman extra friendly, but both owners came out and we got triple-teamed and crushed under a hailstorm of "try this on" and "these are great" coming from all sides. Sure, the store rented equipment, but I don't recall hearing anything about that. We were too busy buying multiple $400 items and enough junk to send the owners on vacation for the rest of the summer.

"So, let's see," one of the owners said in a delightfully friendly voice. "First you need backpacks. Let's take a look. Ooh, this one is one of my favorites. It's really big and you'll find plenty of room in there for whatever you want to bring." From his perspective on packs, bigger is better. Why sell an overnight pack that's on the small end for a measly $250 when there's one big enough to hike to Mars and back for $450? Sold! For $450 to the gentleman who doesn't know that the bigger the pack, the more uncomfortable it will be. "Yes, feels fine," said my dad, having never tried on an overnight pack. "We're going to need one for my son, too." Sold! For $350 to the gentleman with the clueless son.

Next came the sleeping bag. I already had one I think, although I'm not sure why. We needed to buy one more for my dad. "I just want one that's not too hot. I get real hot when I sleep, even when it's cold out." Well, temperature-wise my dad got himself a good one; however, it was a North Face synthetic (as opposed to goose down) that was big, heavy, and impossible to stuff into the small sack that comes with it. All in all it was one of the worst sleeping bags I've ever seen in a nice outdoor store, and we bought it for over $200.

After that we moved on to the tent. It was a doozie. A nice three-man freestanding tent made by Mountain Hardwear. We wanted, or thought we wanted, a three-man with a huge vestibule. It would be nice to have some extra space, right? What I can't get over is how nice it was to carry an extra two pounds on my back every step of the way for roughly 25,000 footsteps. Two pounds isn't too big of a deal, but neither is some extra tent space. Of course extra tent equals extra money for the store, so that was the tent for us. Sold! For $400, to the gentleman who will carry more weight, all day every day, just to have the added comfort of extra tent space. Little does he know that even though he has extra space, he is doomed to be uncomfortable anyway because he's used to sleeping in a big fluffy bed every night.

Moving right along, next was the water filter. Water filters are a necessity for us chlorinated Americans, but since buying the first water filter, I've found cheaper and much better ones. Anyway, we bought the store's top water filter (the highest-priced one at least) for over $100. Next came the stove. It gives me great pain to think about this one.

"Now this, sir, is our finest stove. The fuel is refillable, it is easy to use, and it even comes with this little aluminum wind shield for maximum fuel efficiency."

"Wow, and it's easy to use, you say?"

"Oh yes sir, it's no problem. I use this same stove. The fuel refills are much cheaper than other stoves too." This guy was really suffering from denial after making the same mistake that we did.

So we bought it, another $80, when the same stove I use today by choice was sitting right next to it for $29.95. It's easy to look at backpacking stuff like you would all other consumer products. "Huh, we might as well get the best one. It only costs a little bit more. Besides, the other one that only costs 29 bucks must be really crappy." Not the case at all with some backpacking gear. The expensive things usually turn out to have a bunch of gadgets and accessories that you will never use, and they will just be bothersome. Sure, that $80 stove would have worked better than mine in 70-mile-per-hour winds or at 20,000 feet, but I've never camped in 70-mile-per-hour winds or at 20,000 feet in over a hundred trips, nor do I have a desire to. Believe it or not, cheap in backpacking terms can mean simple, light, and easy to use.

"What kind of socks do you have?"

"Socks?" I said.

"Yes, it's important that you have good hiking socks or you could get blisters. Here try these."

"These are nice, Matt. I'm going to get some, too. We're going to be out for four days so let's go ahead and get four pairs each."

You may be under the impression that hiking socks are cheap. Hmmm, 10–15 bucks a pair—I don't think so. Yes, that's right, we'd already spent $1,400, and now we were buying $100 worth of socks?! Oh boy. Holy "buying four candle lanterns," that's absurd! $1,500 down and we hadn't even been hit by the hurricane of headlamps, batteries, poop shovel, compass, maps, plastic water jug, water bottles, water bottle holders, extra stuff sacks, outdoor kitchen set, pots, frying pans, rain pants, long underwear, thick plastic utensils, pot holder, teacups, bowls, plates, first-aid kit, sunscreen, bug repellent, biodegradable soap, waterproof matches, and last but not least, candle lanterns—one for every color of a rainbow.

It was finally time to go, but not before one more ridiculous question from my dad. "Hey, are these dehydrated meals any good?" Hmmm, let's see, they've sold us on every single thing in the store. What's the harm in saying that they're great?

"Oooh, they're delicious. I love this chili."

"What about the Santa Fe black bean…"

"Wonderful, one of my favorites."

"And is this chocolate cheese…"

"The German chocolate cheesecake? Oh it's really good. I had it on a trip last summer and loved it."

Before you know it, my dad had another 30 bucks worth of crap tucked under his arm. We easily topped $2,000. It's embarrassing to think about, and certainly to write about, but hey, it's in the past, never to be done again, and hopefully I'll save many others from having the same perilous fate. If you happen to have bought this book as part of your epic "first-trip" shopping spree, make sure to locate your receipt immediately and take as much of it back as possible. More importantly, if you have tons of money to throw away, please buy 10 copies of this book instead and give them to friends and family, or just write me a check in the amount that you saved by reading this next section. It's only fair. Right everybody? Right? Hey?

CHAPTER 1

SHOPPING FOR EQUIPMENT

(FOR THE FIRST TIME)

Equipment fits into two categories, essential and nonessential. If you're a first-time backpacker, you really don't know whether a nonessential item is worth carrying or not. I suggest buying the absolute essentials only, and bringing what you missed having on the next trip, like a lantern or a stove. This saves you a lot of time, money, and headache that is associated with figuring out your first backpacking trip. Plus, the worst part about most people's first trips is carrying huge amounts of weight. It is extremely important to keep your load at a minimum. This not only increases fun, it reduces pain and risk of injury. Your body isn't used to carrying heavy loads over rough mountain terrain, so it's very easy to hurt your back, knees, or ankles. Most importantly, a light first load boosts your chances at returning for a second trip.

All you have to do is concentrate on the essentials. Don't let someone else decide what you need and don't need. I'll help you in the rest of this chapter to come up with a shopping list/checklist. Then when you go into the store, focus on buying what's on the list, and that only. Everything else you can ignore.

The essentials include shelter, backpack, clothing, food, and water. Everything else you don't need to survive. You might decide after a little experience with backpacking that it would be nice to have a few nonessentials, and that carrying them won't be a problem. Just don't make the mistake of buying everything you can imagine wanting, filling up your backpack with pounds of these nonessentials, and then lugging them around on your first trip. Make your first trip a light one and decide later if you can handle a little extra weight.

SHELTER

Your essential shelter includes something to keep you dry and something to keep you warm—a tent and a sleeping bag. If you're in the mountains anywhere on earth, you can expect summertime temperatures to drop to near freezing or lower at night, even on the hottest day of the year. So be prepared.

Let's start with the tent—the almighty symbol of outdoor recreation. Personally, I think the best way to buy a tent, and perhaps other gear now that I think about it, is over the Internet. Yes I know, some crazy hacker is going to get your credit card number and ruin your life. Well, be careful, but let's not kid ourselves. Buying gear online is easy, and you don't have any pressure to "buy this here $700 Bibler tent." You actually get to read about what the tent is intended to be used for according to the manufacturer, and there are several gear review websites out there too. Of course there are thousands of people out there that really care and know their stuff when it comes to the latest gear. This you can't find online, so it might be best to inquire in person at your local outdoor store before jumping into anything, but study up before you embark.

Although gear is always changing, there are some generalizations that can be made. The two major criteria to look for in tents are size and seasons. Each tent is designed to fit a certain number of people (usually one to four), and each is designed to accommodate either three seasons (the missing season being winter) or four seasons. To figure out what you need, you have to think about what you will be using the tent for. Will you ever camp in the winter? Will you be going by yourself often? Will you be going in groups of three often? If you're still not sure, that's okay. I'll go over the pros and cons of each type.

The best tent for most people's needs is a simple two-person, three-season tent. It should, unless you are overly claustrophobic, work well for you, another person, and all of your stuff. It's the one-size-almost-fits-all tent. Most reliable tents in this category are cheap, light, easy to set up, etc. For the average wilderness beast ("Wilderbeast") like yourself, it's probably perfect. If you are weird or feel like doing something that you've only seen on a Mountain Dew commercial, then you might want to consider something different. Generally speaking, the following list is what's offered by most tent-making companies:

SIZE
Bivy sacks

These aren't really tents. They are supposedly-waterproof bags that go around your sleeping mat and bag and zip up. Not for the claustrophobic, but if you want to go the ultimate lightweight way, then try a bivy sack. They're actually pretty cool and quite warm. They're fun when it rains. You stay dry (sometimes) while you feel raindrops tickling your whole body. Overall, these are probably a little intimidating for a first-timer, but don't rule them out forever. A few solo trips will perk your interest.

One-man tents

I love these tents, but remember, I am without a doubt, weird. They are small, warm, and absurdly light. The downside is that they are meant for one person, which means that they are only useful for solo trips. No matter how antisocial you are, you'll inevitably want to go with someone other than yourself. So keep that in mind before buying a specialized tent like this.

Two-man tents

Like I said before, these are the most versatile of all. Per person—assuming there will be two of you—they are even lighter than one-mans. If you plan to camp with strangers, it might be a bit small. You will be lying shoulder to shoulder and almost always up against, on top of, underneath, or getting breathed on by the person you are with. This may sound terrifying, but you'll get used to it. If you're confident that you won't ever, no matter what, get used to these kinds of sleeping conditions, buy yourself a one-man and sleep at a safe distance from your companions—especially if they have very infectious diseases or lice. In all seriousness, you would need a damn good list of reasons to convince me that a two-man tent *isn't* the best kind for you to buy.

Three-man tents

The first tent ever purchased by my family was a three-man. It was purchased with the idea that some time my mother would come with me and my dad. We also decided that a little extra space in the tent would be much more comfortable. It was comfortable no doubt, but after years of experience I've come to discover weight to play a bigger role in comfort. So, this three-man is now in storage. For $200 (instead of $400) I bought a two-man Marmot tent. It works great. It's warmer, easier to set up and take down, 30% lighter, and about half the size when it's all packed up. But you must make the call. If you're planning on going in groups of three often, and none of you want to sleep alone, then a three-man is something to consider, and for a few extra pounds and $100, you can have a lot of extra space.

Four-man tents and beyond

As far as I'm concerned, these are very specialized tents. The only time I can see it being worth the money is on a huge expedition with a lot of people, or a trip where you plan on spending several days at a time in your tent (i.e., climbing Everest). Even under those circumstances, there is also the fart issue to think about. If each ass in the tent farts approximately five times per night, then the more people sleeping in the tent the more farts you must endure. In a two-man, based on the five-fart-per-night theory, you only have to deal with an average of five farts other than your own each night. In a six-man expedition tent you're looking at 25, and that number can increase exponentially depending on what was served for dinner. If you need tent space for four or more, use multiple two-man tents instead of cramming yourselves into one big four-man. I just don't think you'll be able to fill a four-man on many trips—making the excess tent excess weight.

SEASONS

Three-season tents

These tents are the best option for you unless you plan to go winter camping often. Three-season tents have thinner walls and better air circulation—typically. They are also a couple of pounds lighter and quite a bit cheaper. If you plan to do 90% summer backpacking or more, a three-season tent is the best for you.

Four-season tents

They sound so much tougher, like they could remain standing through a blizzard, a hurricane, a tornado. Four-season tents *are* tougher. They are also tougher to pay for and carry. Like I mentioned before, if you're serious about winter camping, then it's a good investment. If not, forget about it. Besides, a three-season tent will be fine in winter if the weather is relatively mild and you've got a warm sleeping bag. I've comfortably survived many zero to ten-degree nights in my three-season tent.

RELIABLE MANUFACTURERS

Well, this is a tough one. Everyone seems to have their own opinion of what's good and what is the most hideous piece of junk on earth. So here are my opinions that were somehow mysteriously shaped and formed through a combination of experiences, stories, and advice from others—just like most opinions. Not all brands are listed, just the ones I have any familiarity with at all. Take them with a grain of salt.

Low price, low quality
- Eureka!
- Coleman

Low price, average quality
- Cabella's

Low price, high quality—Dream on!

Average price, average quality
- Sierra Designs
- Moss
- Kelty
- The North Face

Average price, high quality
- Marmot
- Mountain Hardwear

Highest price, best (but excessive) quality
- Bibler

One thing I must mention is that these manufacturers change sporadically. The market is all about reputation. Once a good reputation is established, it's not uncommon for the manufacturer to take a shortcut here or there. This trend is most blatantly obvious with the company The North Face. They've been around for ages and were considered to be the leader in outdoor equipment for decades. In the mid to late '90s they cut back quality and left tremendous price tags on their gear. With mediocre gear on the market and exorbitant price tags, I rebelled against them, verbally bashed them every chance I got, and even went so far to put a North Face sticker on the shovel I use to dig poopholes while I'm out. They are being forced to compete again, and hey, I just bought a North Face tent. The point is that the above manufacturer labels I've dished out may become totally untrue at any moment. These companies are always playing leapfrog, so ask around and see what kind of vibe you get on which company is currently making the gear with the best value.

OTHER THINGS TO CONSIDER

There are a few more missing details that you should be aware of. First of all, look at the size of the vestibule. The vestibule is the area outside of the tent that is covered by the rainfly. The bigger the better if it isn't making the tent significantly heavier.

Another thing is making the choice between a tent that is or is not "freestanding." Freestanding tents stand up by themselves without having to stake them down. These are very convenient if you are camping on rock surfaces or frozen ground, but they are heavier. I've tried both and I've dealt with both inconveniences—extra weight and not being able to get your stakes into the ground. I'd say the lightest freestanding tent on the market would be your overall favorite.

Also shop for a tent that has a sloped shape as you look at it from the outside. This helps to let rain slide off the top instead of puddle up. Staying dry is the main thing, and all tents are supposed to be waterproof—the ones that let gravity help work the best as far as I've experienced.

Finally, check the size. The taller and wider the better. A tent that is too short to sit up in can be slightly annoying, but it's obviously not of life-and-death importance.

SLEEPING BAG

The other essential item under the shelter category is the ol' sleeping bag. At first, a sleeping bag is a real pain in the ass. You flop around inside of them, wiggling like you're in a straightjacket. Getting tangled up in one will make you crazy enough to need a straightjacket, too. It's a claustrophobic struggle—one that everyone who has slept in a sleeping bag can relate to, especially when it comes time to go to the bathroom in the middle of the night. You're tired, it's cold out, and you finally give up on trying to hold it in at the last minute—leaving yourself with a frantic half minute to get out of the bag before your bladder explodes. "My zipper's stuck ... ah c'mon ... I've really gotta pee ... Goddammit! Help!"

Unfortunately, the more cocoonlike your sleeping bag is, the warmer it will probably be. That's why having a sense of humor about getting stuck in a tangled sleeping bag—its zipper caught on part of your bag, or even worse, your sleeve—is important. So let's talk about what kind of sleeping bag will best fit your needs.

TEMPERATURE RATINGS

It's easy to be too intimidated or not intimidated enough about overnight temps in the high country. Of course, I'm assuming you will be camping in the most common place for people to camp—some alpine mountain range—but if you will be backpacking in Florida, this section probably won't make much sense.

As I was saying, it's easy to misjudge how warm of a sleeping bag you will need. The most important thing to consider is what kind of sleeper you are at home. If you can't stand being too cold, then you might want to go on the warmer side. If you sweat without clothes or covers with the window open like I do, then you might want to go on the lighter side. Regardless of what you buy, you'll probably still be too hot or too cold or both at some point. They haven't created a sleeping bag with a thermostat yet, and unlike your bedroom, car, and office—the temperature sometimes changes more than five degrees. Oh no!

Sleeping bags are sold with certain temperature ratings, which are never true, but they do give you an idea. A good summer-only sleeping bag should have a temperature rating of somewhere between 10 and 35 degrees F. Any warmer or colder and you might have some uncomfortable nights. To let you know the limits, I've slept in a 35-degree bag in 20 degrees and been warm. I've also seen people with 15-degree bags get cold at 25 or 30 degrees. Personally, I think getting a bag with a rating somewhere between 15 and 25 degrees will get you through even the coldest summer mountain night. If you do plan on winter camping with it and don't want to buy two bags—one for each season, you could go as low as 0 degrees and probably get away with it. You can always unzip it and use it more like a blanket on a hot night, but warmer bags are significantly heavier.

SIZE AND WEIGHT

When buying a sleeping bag, you also have to consider size and weight. Not every sleeping bag is designed for backpacking. Many are designed for car camping. They might have the temperature rating that you're looking for but weigh five pounds and look like a baby elephant in a sack strapped to your backpack. Most cheap car-camping bags are easy to point out. They look like two blankets sewn together. That's not what you want. You want a bag that is shaped like a cocoon (they are called "mummy" bags). Even the heavy-duty ones don't weigh much more than three pounds. The average summer bag weighs a little over two—less if you're lucky.

QUALITY

Yes, back to the topic of quality brands. I would go with a Marmot, Mountain Hardwear, or Western Mountaineering brand bag. I also wouldn't rule out a Sierra Designs or Kelty bag, although I can't speak from experience on either of those two brands. I used Marmot sleeping bags for a decade, and they were fantastic, but nothing compares to a Western Mountaineering bag. They are made with the highest-quality fabrics and highest-quality down, meaning they are the lightest, smallest, warmest, most comfortable, and most pricey. It's all about the quality of the goose down. The higher the fill number, the better the bag.

COMFORT

It's a little bit of an oxymoron for a beginning backpacker—comfort, that is. There are basically two kinds of sleeping bags to buy: down and synthetic.

Down is by far the best for a number of reasons—it's light, it's comfortable, and it can be compacted more than synthetic; however, down is much higher-maintenance. First of all, you can't get it wet or it's useless. It sounds scary, but you just have to keep it in a dry place and not do anything stupid—easier said than done. You also can't store it all stuffed up in its stuff sack for more than a few days. It will ruin it. Third, it costs a hell of a lot more. Why buy it then? Because I said so. Down sleeping bags are incredible—definitely worth the extra bucks. Just take care of it.

One more thing—sleeping bags usually come in sizes—short, regular, and long (5'6, 6'0, and 6'6, respectively). Don't get the large for extra space and comfort; they are bigger and heavier.

SON OF A ... !

You went out, it was a balmy 45 degrees, and you shivered all night. Don't run out and buy another bag that's warmer. Make sure that you're doing all that you can do to stay warm.

- Wear a ski hat when you sleep
- Use a sleeping pad—the fatter the warmer
- Tighten the drawstring at the top (if you have one) so that it closes in around your head and seals off cold air from invading
- Keep your tent zipped up
- Sleep in yer birthday suit. Clothes shield the radiation of heat between your 98-degree flesh and the bag. Just don't let any cold air in.
- Buy a sleeping bag liner—these are usually made of silk. They look pathetic but they really work at adding a few degrees to your body while you sleep (only buy one of these after you've used the bag to find out how effective it is—don't pull a "might as well buy one just in case" stunt—there's a 99% chance that you'll be fine if you do all of the other things on the list).

FINDING A BACKPACK

I can't honestly say that I'm an expert on backpacks. A backpack expert would own a backpack that is perfectly comfortable and practical in every way—and I don't. I've had little luck with finding one that is truly comfortable—but I can give a good explanation for why this is true. Back in the days of the first epic shopping trip, my dad bought a gargantuan Osprey Zenith backpack that has since been handed down to me. It's a great pack, but it is absolutely huge. It's meant for a trip with a ridiculous amount of stuff. It's great for desert trips where you must carry all of your water—usually several gallons per person. It's also great for long treks lasting several weeks, where there is no place to resupply. Otherwise, it sucks. It is painful and awkward, and nine out of ten trips, I wish I had something smaller. So what I recommend is going small. Really small. As small as you can possibly go without having to leave essential items behind. Small packs are, you guessed it, lighter and cheaper.

Backpacks are measured in cubic feet or liters. Recently I downsized to a pack with about a 4,500-cubic-inch (75-liter) capacity. In the backpack world, this is known as a weekend or long weekend size. I can easily get two weeks out of it, and you should be able to also. There's no real reason to go over 90 liters unless you are just a sick, pain-loving, masochistic bastard.

There are all kinds of brands of backpacks, and I don't really think there is a best and worst. There's Gregory, Osprey, The North Face, Kelty, Arc'Teryx, and a bunch more. Unfortunately, trying them on is all but pointless, especially if you've never tried a backpack on before. "Uh, sure, it feels fine stuffed with newspapers. How does it feel with 40 pounds in it after 12 miles?" There's no way you or the greatest backpack expert on earth can figure out how it's going to feel until you've given it the true field test. The only test you can give it at a store is to load it up with some weight, and adjust it the best you can. You want the weight to be evenly distributed. You want the shoulder straps to be in full contact with your shoulders. You want the hip belt to be 100% comfortable. The most important thing is that the frame fits your torso. If it's too long or too short, you'll have real problems with no solution. A pack is definitely not something to buy online. Try on every one in every store, come up with a tedious list of pros and cons of each pack, and don't rush into a decision. Just remember, buying a backpack on the small end will increase your chances of being comfortable. Most importantly, try to find a salesperson who really knows what he or she is talking about, is willing to adjust pack after pack to help you find the best for you, and really seems interested in helping you find your best fit.

Also pay attention to accessories. Buy something with a good set of straps on the outside. That way you can really get away with using a small pack—if you can't fit everything inside, you can start throwing stuff on the outside. Also make sure that there is a good spot for your sleeping bag. This is your most cherished item, and you need to fit it inside for extra rain and "falling on your back crossing a stream" protection. If you plan on carrying hiking poles or a fishing pole, or anything extra on the outside, make sure your pack has the straps to accommodate them—or a nice place to put additional straps (you can buy them separately). Also, most packs come with detachable sections for day hikes away from camp. These really come in handy. Finally, and probably most importantly, buy a pack with padded shoulder straps, a large padded hip belt, and another strap that clips across the chest. You'll be miserable if you are missing any one of these components.

CLOTHING

This is the easy part, but listen to my advice. I promise I know what I'm talking about. Remember, I'm an obsessive backpacker and I'm really nit-picky about what I bring, but this is a product of experience. After years of changing my mind and trying new things out, I think I've finally come up with the perfect clothing arsenal for mountainous conditions. Again, this may not apply to you if you're planning a desert hike in August or a backpacking trip on Kauai.

THE TOP

On top you need something light to hike in, something warm, and something rainproof. First of all, you're not packing for a vacation. You don't have to look cool and mix up your wardrobe every day. You are dressing for the weather, packing clothes that will be light. That means one of each—maybe two on the T-shirts at most. Yes, you might have to become a little pigpen for a few days, but remember, more than half of the people in the world wash their clothes outside in the river anyway. Life goes on without a washing machine. Life does exist outside of your walk-in closet.

For the light hiking T-shirt, I suggest buying two fancy fast-drying Capilene ones at the outdoor store if you've got some extra cash. Patagonia and Mountain Hardwear make some pretty sweet ones. If not, you'll survive just fine with a couple of dirt- and sweat-collecting cotton T-shirts from your drawer. Remember though—just two. More than two and you might as well be on a cruise ship.

For something warm, I would bring a fairly thick fleece jacket. This will be your pillow and the main layer that keeps you warm when the temperature drops 45 degrees or so as the sun goes down. Just one. See if you can impart your signature scent on that puppy before the end of the first trip.

Lastly on the top, you need a rain jacket. This is the most important article of clothing. Make sure it is a damn good one. One that is double-layered and a little heavier is probably a good idea. You know when I tell you that it's better to get the heavier one that it's pretty important. Dry upper body—good; hypothermia, which more people die of in the summer than the winter—bad.

The only other thing you might need is a down vest for extra warmth if you're expecting extra-cold spring or autumn temperatures. If it's going to fall below freezing, you'll want more than just a fleece unless you plan on spending a lot of time in your sleeping bag.

THE BOTTOM

Let's start at the very bottom. You need something on your feet. Personally, I only bring one pair of shoes with me most of the time. I've hiked enough miles with water squishing out of them that I just don't really care about having dry feet anymore. Your feet, if you're in the mountains, will get wet—ballerinas and clumsy ogres alike. Mud, little streams, rain, etc. Gore-Tex? Probably not enough. So don't worry about getting the stuff that's the ultimate in waterproofness. Get the lightest-weight medium-cut or high-top boot in the store (the huge heavy-duty ones are for people who like 200 miles of blisters and need to lift an extra couple pounds with every footstep for extra exercise), and bring a pair of really light, comfortable, foot-relaxing, camp shoes—and keep 'em dry. Also buy a pair of those really cool outdoor sandals if you like stopping every hour or two, taking your boots and socks off, cutting your feet on sharp rocks in river crossings, and putting boots and socks back on over your wet bloody feet—then hiking several more miles over rocky, muddy terrain, getting your boots wet anyway.

You also need socks. Yes, you probably already have socks, too many of them, but cotton whities won't cut it. Backpacking socks are really expensive. One good pair costs about the same as a 12-pack of your standard Target crew socks. They really are essential though. Blisters are more miserable than you can ever imagine, and the type of socks you wear makes a huge difference—although even a $20 pair of hiking socks won't make you immune to them. Some people like wool socks, but I can't stand them. They itch and they don't have the elastic goodness that keeps them formed to your foot perfectly for several days at a time. Two pairs of these backpacking socks are all you need—one to wear while the other one dries. You might want to bring three pairs, but forget trying to bring a fresh pair for every day of a two-week trip. Like I said before, it is possible to wash clothes without a washing machine. Amazing!

Working our way up, next comes the pants. You need some long pants. Rain pants aren't as essential as some warm fleece pants for camp, but they can be nice to have in a real downpour. Do make sure that you have one or the other. Personally, I like to wear long pants a lot while I'm hiking. Many trails are overgrown with vegetation, and at times you will hike with little trail at all. Long pants protect the legs from little scratches and stuff. On the other hand, little scratches on you calves and shins look really tough. It's your call, but like I said, bring one pair of warm pants—waterproof or not. Leave those red Wrangler's at home, cowgirl. Fleece—good. Tight denim—uh, not so much.

Shorts. That almighty symbol of freedom from your desk-jockeying duties. These are great to bring. One pair is plenty. Light-weight, quick-drying shorts are the best, but any will do.

Your undies are your call. For long trips, two pairs should be fine. Rotate them like you do your socks and T-shirts. Wear one pair while you wash the other.

FOOD AND BEVERAGE

Okay chef. Here's what I have to say about backcountry cooking for a first-timer. Don't do it. If you do, keep it simple. Yes I said *don't cook*—that's not synonymous with *don't eat*. Bring some sandwiches for the first day. Some bagels and cream cheese for the next. Some beef jerky, some Granola, a couple of candy bars, some cheese and crackers, and some raisins. It sounds pathetic, but the last thing you need to be buying and fooling around with on your first trip is a bunch of outdoor cookwear. If you must eat hot food and have tea, bring a little pot, some hot dogs, buns, s'more goodies, and do it over an open fire if that's allowed at your destination. You can even toast your cold dry bagel over the campfire in the morning if you need to. You don't need to fool with camp stoves and dehydrated stuff your first time out, I promise.

If you are the type that isn't turned on by the thought of sleeping outdoors, but outdoor stoves have always looked like so much fun that you wanted to try backpacking, then give it a whirl, and for God's sake—buy the cheapest one in the store. The double pump-action Himalaya Extremely Extreme Extremeness Titanium XPS 2000 is *extremely* unnecessary for an average backpacker. Start simple with some Top Ramen. Try the stove out on some hot chocolate, oatmeal, and other easy things. If you really insist on going gourmet on your first trip, then flip to Part IV for guidance.

WATER

Now we're getting serious. You need this stuff and you need it every day. Mountain stream water is the freshest, cleanest water on earth—if it's filtered first. Although sometimes it will seem unlikely that some crystal-clear stream will make you sick, don't screw around. Filter it. How? With a backpacking water purifier. It sounds elaborate, but it's really not. You drop a tube in the water and pump, and water goes straight into your water bottle to slowly but surely form the best bottle of water you'll ever have—a hard-earned bottle of water, and there is no nuclear waste dump between the creek's headwaters and where you're standing—unless you've made some very poor decisions in your planning process. Fresh water is a beautiful thing. Kool-Aid mix has no place in your backpack. Please let your body enjoy at least a few quarts of perfect, pure liquid.

Water purifiers come in all shapes, sizes, and of course, prices. The major brands that I'm most familiar with are MSR, Pur, First Need, Sweetwater, and a couple of others. Stick to these brands. These are ones you can trust, and when I say "trust," I'm talking "suck down a big glass of filtered toilet water" trust. I used to use a reasonably priced MSR filter. It worked, but was difficult and tedious to use. You'll be pumping water more quickly with expensive models like a First Need. Santa brought me one of those this year. I could go toe to toe with a firehose with that thing. For crisp, clean, mountain water, you can feel safe with any purifier. For Third World swamp water, buy the purifier that filters the smallest particles.

Your two other options are to carry in all of your water—the most economical way to backpack unless you take the post-trip knee surgery expenses into account—or buy iodine tablets. Iodine tablets are cheap and much lighter than water filters. They also make your pristine mountain water not so pristine. In fact, they make it about as pristine and flavorful as a mouthful of water from the baby pool. Personally, I carry the extra weight of a water filter. Once again, please note that this item is important enough to sacrifice some extra weight. If I say it's worth carrying, it's probably worth it. Iodine tablets are better to bring in the first-aid kit for emergency reasons—in case your filter clogs or breaks (has never happened to me in probably over 1,000 gallons of filtered water, but you never know when it will).

So the essentials are now covered—shelter, clothing, backpack, food, and water. In the next chapter I discuss many, but not all, of the possible accessories on the market. You will definitely want a few of these items, but please, try to stick to the essentials as best as you can. You will survive, and believe it or not, sometimes it's more fun the less you have. It's just one of those things that reminds you that you're not at the office, you're doing something different, you're on an adventure. I love to be able to experience what a human's life should feel like—a life without cars and smog and noise and McDonald's and the daily "who got blown up" news report. It's true freedom. Freedom from your possessions and your worries. Most importantly, bringing less with you helps you see that there is a world and a way of living other than the one you've seen all your life.

CHAPTER 2

WHO NEEDS IT?

Who needs it? The answer is no one, but many of the following items are darn close to essential. So close that you may feel that they are necessary to your survival. Backpacking stores are full of all kinds of accessories, gadgets, and garbage that you must sort your way through. You can't bring them all, although a good salesman can easily sell them all. A salesman is supposedly an expert, and perhaps you aren't. All he or she has to say is, "Do you have one of these? Oh, you've gotta have one of these," and you've been hooked. Come up with a plan of attack before getting within a quarter mile of an outdoor store. If you don't, bring home all of your purchases in a cardboard box so you can take it directly to your storage unit, where it will sit for all eternity.

GO-GO GADGETS

Here comes a list of gadgets and accessories that actually could be of some use. You won't need all of them, that's for sure, but the items in this list will at least be something to consider. Many of these items I own and bring with me. Use this list to make a checklist of your very own. I'm not going to make one for you and tell you what to bring. It's your choice. Remember, you can survive without any of these items. Don't forget to add tent, sleeping bag, food, water filter, clothes, and backpack to your checklist!

HEADLAMPS

These are pretty cool. I don't know why it took so long, but they finally came up with headlamps that are tiny. Don't buy one of the huge ones. It's way too much weight for such a minor accessory. Petzl has long been the leading brand and you can trust that their products will work just fine, but there are several others out there that may suit you better.

STOVES

I'll get more into this in "Dining Out," but yes, a stove is a good thing to have, especially for long trips where weight can be saved by bringing large amounts of dried food and rehydrating them later using your stove and a light-weight camping pot.

POTS AND PANS

Well, yes if you're bringing a stove, duh. How about some fuel for your stove too while you're at it.

EATING UTENSILS

I usually bring a couple of sturdy plastic forks and spoons. They sell these at most camping stores. Chopsticks can be useful too. Yes, they make ultra-light titanium utensils. And you thought I was obsessed!

SPADE

Better known as "poop shovel." Yes, please bring one of these—a plastic one to save weight. They can break but only cost a couple of bucks to replace.

TOILET PAPER

A lot of people can do without. Some can't. Don't be afraid to try the left-hand splash technique. More and more areas are making people pack out their used toilet paper. And you think I'm disgusting for using a handful of water to do the job? Nothing a little Dr. Bronner's peppermint soap can't fix. (My mom's going to tell everyone I was adopted after reading this.)

POCKET KNIFE

I always bring some kind of Swiss Army knife or Leatherman. I've used them for at least a dozen different things over the years, the most important being to fix broken tent poles.

LIGHTER OR MATCHES

I like to bring at least two lighters. One plastic Bic lighter and one naked lady whose nipples glow when I light it. Hey, I get pretty lonely out there.

FIRST-AID KIT

I have trouble believing that a first-aid kit could reverse the outcome of a life-and-death situation, but everyone says it's smart to bring one, so I do. I just like having Band-Aids and Neosporin, maybe a couple of Advil, and a blister kit.

BLISTER KIT

Bring one. There are all different kinds. I like to bring a large selection. Some people prefer duct tape. I just don't like the really thick Moleskin. It always gets rubbed off right away.

BUG JUICE

I never bring this stuff, but many sissies can't handle the terrifying thought of forgetting it. I'd rather get bitten by mosquitoes than put some toxic, foul-smelling, God-awful-tasting chemical all over my body. Uh, I guess I'm sounding a bit on the sissy side myself. Weigh the pros and cons for yourself.

MAPS

Always bring a map of the area you're in, even if you know your way around.

COMPASS

Figure out how to use one and bring it with you. A map is only slightly more than useless without one. (There is an entire section on map and compass orienteering in Chapter 15.)

ROPE/STRING

I like to bring a little twine or string with me. It's good for hanging food and stretching out the rainfly on your tent perfectly.

SOLAR SHOWER

It seems hard to believe that I recommend bringing one of these, but I think they have a purpose when used to lessen the impact that you have on your campsite, but an empty milk jug might be all you need.

BIODEGRADABLE SOAP

It's a good idea to bring a little for washing pots and pans, your hands, etc. Also good for washing clothes and hair. Dr. Bronner's makes the best multi-purpose soap.

TOOTHBRUSH AND TOOTHPASTE

Don't forget this one when traveling with others.

CONTACT LENSES

If you wear contact lenses and refuse to go without, don't forget them or your saline.

OTHER TOILETRIES

Bring them, but go lighter if possible. Take a smaller bottle or pack just enough to get you through in a plastic bag.

EXTRA STUFF SACKS

I don't know if they call them stuff sacks because you put "stuff" in them or because you "stuff" things in them, but they are great for food and other items. They are light, make your pack more organized, and are water-resistant.

KITCHEN KITS

These are great organizing sacks, but if you're tight for money don't get one. OR (Outdoor Research) makes the "Outdoor Kitchen," which I've used for years.

SUNGLASSES

Always.

HAT

I usually bring one to help shield the sun, and to keep the raindrops from smacking me in the face.

SKI HAT

A nice wool or fleece hat is good for cold mornings and nights.

GLOVES

Sometimes it gets really cold, but you'll probably be fine without them.

SUNSCREEN

Mountain sunlight, endless hours of it, can be pretty rough, but hey, if you want to get skin cancer, then you can speed up the process by leaving the sunscreen at home.

WATER BOTTLES

At least two in an area where there are plenty of streams to refill them often. If you're out in the desert, bring multiple gallon containers—you might only be able to refill once a week.

BOOK OR JOURNAL

It's nice to have one or the other, but it's obviously not required for survival.

CAMERA

It's not like you're really going to capture the true beauty of a place with a camera. Ansel Adams couldn't even do it, and you think you can? I know you'll bring one anyway. You're just like all the others. I am easily annoyed by small gadgets, but don't you forget this one and try to actually remember to bring film or your flash card and battery if you're "digital." Just don't get too wrapped up in it. Cameras will undoubtedly lessen your wilderness experience.

HIKING POLES/HIKING STICK

If you have knee problems or plan on carrying a pack so gigantic that you need extra balance support, then please, try these out. They may really come in handy. But remember, if humans needed hiking poles that badly, we would have all been born with four legs. I've never needed them.

GAITERS

Good for hiking in snow. Bring some if you really think there's a need.

GPS (GLOBAL POSITIONING SYSTEM)

They're awesome if you've got extra money and can handle complex gadgetry. For a long time I resisted them, but they're simply incredible. I rarely leave home without one anymore. Be warned, however, that if you don't have a firm grasp on map and compass skills, do not use one. It'll confuse you until you get lost. Typing in one wrong coordinate or making one false assumption will get you into trouble. It sounds almost like I've done that half a dozen times, doesn't it? Hmmm, coincidence I guess.

There really are an almost infinite number of frivolous items sold at backpacking stores that you must be careful to avoid. The idea is to sucker the people who want all of the luxuries of their three-bedroom homes in the backcountry. The people who try to achieve that must really suffer, carrying a load that a horse would injure itself carrying, finding out in the end that the only place like their three-bedroom home *is* their three-bedroom home. Backpacking is altogether a completely different lifestyle for a few days or more. Trying to make it filled with all the conveniences of Western society is painfully impossible. That's painful *and* impossible. It's all about attitude. Go light and simple and you'll have a much better time. Give up on making it perfect and convenient and find a way to enjoy the buzzing of mosquitoes in your ears, the squishing of wet socks under your feet, and the aching coldness in your rear as you sit on a jagged rock by a stream.

PART II

WHERE TO?

There's something about a national park that sucks you in
like a vacuum.

The park may be fully surrounded by amazing trails, gorgeous remote mountain ranges, untouched streams—but a national park will make you overlook all that. Is it the name? You've heard it, you've seen pictures, you drove through there as a kid with your parents in the ol' RV. Is it because it shows up better on the atlas? Is it because the paved roads take you right through there? Is it all the signs that point you toward them from all directions? What the hell is it? It takes guts to choose a no-name wilderness area in the middle of a vaguely outlined national forest when you're surrounded by dozens of national parks. But sometimes that's what you've gotta do—especially in the midst of the massive outdoor playground known as California.

I spent a summer living in California as one of its weekend warriors. I had to be choosy. The options were endless. "Hmmm, what am I in the mood for this weekend? Canyons or mountains? Desert or ocean? Snow or sand? Highest point in the lower 48, or the lowest? Oldest tree on earth, tallest tree on earth, or biggest tree on earth? Decisions, decisions." The amazing national parks of California beckoned me, but I resisted with much will power, because I knew there was a better option. And this is what I found.

On the weekend of July 4, perhaps the busiest backpacking weekend of the year in the U.S., I had to bravely face the California crowds. There were at least 300 cars in the parking lot. A shiver of fear tingled up my spine. The nervousness of being trampled to death penetrated my stomach. I was used to seeing less than 300 cars while driving to the trailhead in Colorado, and now I was witnessing 300 at the trailhead. "Dear Lord what have I done?" With head down and pack strapped on, I took off, trying to quickly leave as many of these folks behind as possible, grumbling as I passed noisy family after noisy family.

The trail was everything I had expected, but the farther I made it, the less people I saw. Perhaps I just wasn't noticing as much. It was hard to notice anything besides the tall trees, the wildflowers, and the large peaks on the horizon. After a few short hours, the land flattened a bit, and I sensed that the lake would be coming up soon. I continued along the trail until the forest ended, dramatically revealing the gigantic, shimmering, Aloha Lake. It was a blue ocean of sparkling water surrounded by toothlike peaks capped with snow. Around the lake was an amusement park of boulders. I hopped around like a goofy uncoordinated child that physically had hit puberty, but mentally had not. An occasional "whoop" came out and there was even a *Sound of Music*-esque spin or two. There was much basking in the sun and many "oh my Gods." The big shock was the lack of people. They were condensed along the trail, but the lake was so huge that I seemingly had the whole world to myself.

I put off setting up the tent for hours because playtime kept calling me. By the time I finally got around to it, a large round object had risen in the sky that looked almost identical to the moon, but was much larger and slightly orange. All was silent and calm. Only a slight ripple in the lake nearby uttered a peep. A cool breeze touched me as I stared up at the orange, moonlike sphere in the sky that was rising just above the shadowy black pines on the horizon. The sky behind it was fading from blue to a dark mystical purple. A couple of stars were twinkling high above me. Faster than you can say, "I could cry right now it's so beautiful," I found myself wiping tears from my cheeks and sniffling.

Daylight faded completely as I stood there like a statue, being splashed by the moon as if it were hot sunlight on a cool day. It was an incredible peace— one where the feeling of standing was scarcely different from being sprawled out on a featherbed. Before going to sleep I sipped warm soup, and appreciated the experience in a way that I never had before. And last, but not least, I pulled my sleeping bag from the tent, laid it down on the rock under the sky, and crawled in for a soothing sleep.

By morning my symptoms had not subsided. I hiked all around the area— to other lakes, up mountains, scrambling across rocks. I saw hardly a soul once I'd gotten away from the main trail. After lunch I made the amazing discovery that the shallow water of the lake was actually warm, and I spent hours swimming around through narrow backwater canals.

By late afternoon my gut ached with the thought of leaving. I hadn't wanted to stay somewhere so badly since my first visit to Toys R Us at age eight. "Could I quit my job? Who would worry about me if I didn't come back?" I did the right thing by conservative standards and hiked back to the car, dutifully drove home, and returned to work the next day. The painful week of work was compensated for by my return to Aloha Lake in the Desolation Wilderness the following weekend. I swam in the same water, slept on the same rock, and even ate the same kind of soup for dinner.

What a discovery I had made! Even with the big Independence Day crowds, it was one of the coolest places I'd ever been to. It was far better than seeing El Capitan in Yosemite while choking on exhaust fumes, far better than following paved trails between the world's largest trees in Sequoia National Park, even better than dodging mountain goats in Glacier National Park with the rumble of cars in the distance. It was everything a backpacking trip can be.

Not every adventure can be perfect, but the following chapters are filled with some helpful hints on how to discover places like this for yourself. Wilderness, a type of public land that I will discuss in detail in this section, is usually your best bet for finding a great place to go backpacking, but it's certainly not your only option. Even national parks as crowded as Yosemite and Yellowstone have their hidden backpacking treasures. The key is to thoroughly explore a map of the area. A map can tell you almost all you need to know about your trip and is the ultimate planning guide.

CHAPTER 3

PICKING A PLACE

Unfortunately you can't go backpacking everywhere. You've got to find an interesting area that allows it. That part can be easy or hard depending on where you live. The hard part is choosing. This can be really tough to do in an area you aren't familiar with, and even harder if you've never been backpacking before. How are you supposed to know where the good places are? There's good backpacking in the desert, in the mountains, near the ocean, and in dense forests. The choice is yours. All areas and types of terrain have their own unique beauty and personality.

Your first step is to pick the area where you would like to go. If you live 20 minutes from the Cascades in northern Washington, your decision will be a little easier than for someone living in Iowa. The advantage to living in Iowa (yes, there is one) is that you can choose anyplace, and there is really nothing guiding your decision other than your own curiosities. You can go and explore totally new and different areas each spring, summer, fall, and maybe winter too—and that's what backpacking is all about.

So how do you find out about great places? I've found that being self-sufficient in your search is the best way—as opposed to local guidebooks, trail guides, etc. Most of these books contain a long list of the most popular and accessible hikes, misleading descriptions, and useless maps and photos. In this chapter I'll discuss the different types of backpacking areas, how and what kind of maps to buy, and how to use them efficiently for finding the best possible hike for whatever your backpacking needs may be.

PUBLIC LAND

The land you choose for your trip will most likely be public land, unless you are buddy-buddy with Ted Turner. Three federal agencies in the United

States manage most of this public land: the U.S. Forest Service, the National Parks Service, and the Bureau of Land Management (BLM).

First of all, let's get one thing straight, because many people don't know the difference, or at least get things confused. National forests, national monuments, and national parks are three very different types of public land. National forests are managed by the U.S. Forest Service. National parks and most national monuments are managed by the National Park Service. These three types of land are your best bet for finding a good place to go backpacking. For the most part, BLM land is not considered backpackers' heaven. Most BLM land tends to be the leftovers from the other agencies. Of course you wouldn't rule it out for a potential backpacking trip, especially in the desert states like Utah and Arizona, which have amazing BLM backpacking, but don't travel halfway across the country for a trip there.

National parks, in my opinion, are not the best backpacking spots. They are like giant magnets that attract human flesh from all over the world, sucking them in by the thousands in cars and buses. With the human flesh comes gas stations, hotels, second-rate restaurants, low-quality gift shops, and "much much more for four easy payments of only $19.99." They're like big zoos with openings in the cages for your vehicles to pass through, further penetrating and disrupting an already inadequate amount of habitat for forests and animals to truly live their lives in peace.

The positive side from a backpacker's perspective is that national parks, in general, contain the most beautiful mountains, streams, rock formations, and natural wonders in the country—places so special that they have been given the "honor" and "protection" that our National Park Service provides. Unfortunately, the most spectacular peaks, waterfalls, etc. can be seen from the window of your car. To see them by backpack means to hear the roar of traffic, smell the sour car exhaust, and see the degradation that is a direct result of thousands of people passing through every day.

The list of reasons not to go to a national park continues. With more tourism and more people comes more animal problems. Bears, raccoons, and other inquisitive animals figure out very quickly that humans and food are always in the same place at the same time. If you are backpacking in a national park, then you will rarely be more than 10 miles from the nearest campground. This is a short distance for a hungry bear, and dealing with bear problems can be a real pain—carrying bear canisters, sharing food space with other campers in a steel box (found at many popular national park campsites), and many more headaches, including the slight danger of bears who have lost their instinctual fear of humans.

You might also be unable to get a permit. National parks require backcountry permits, and many of them charge a decent amount of money to get them, too. That has certainly become a pet peeve of mine. My backpacking trips are usually very spontaneous. Planning around an office's hours don't usually jive well with my schedule, and I almost always have to drive out of my way to get there.

Okay, end of tangent. Don't get me wrong. Our country's 60-plus national parks, for the most part, are a good thing. Some parks have very few roads, and the backpacking off the beaten path is outstanding to say the least. Most parks are huge, too—thousands and sometimes millions of acres, with hundreds of miles of trails for me to wear out my shoes on. I'm also glad that they're national parks and not golf courses or cattle ranches. I'm just trying to let out a little frustration and steer you more towards my personal preference—national forests.

Before I get into national forests, let's talk about national monuments. Most national monuments are like miniature national parks. They are usually run by the Park Service and much smaller than your average national park. They are also subject to being disbanded by, say, a certain redneck president that might come Bushwhacking through with plans for oil drilling and mining. Despite their volatile status, they are great places to get away for the weekend and are usually less crowded. In fact, my favorite place to go in the spring and fall is Escalante National Monument in southern Utah.

Okay, back to national forests. My opinions on this topic are most certainly biased. I worked for a few seasons for the Forest Service as a wilderness ranger. I discovered places so pristine and amazingly beautiful that I was blown away. I became a backpacking addict. I had no idea how great backpacking could be, and I owe much of that to White River and Gunnison National Forests in Colorado. How could I recommend anything to you other than to go where I've gone and do what I've done? It couldn't have worked out any better, and my life is forever changed in a very good way. It was here that I discovered what is still my personal preference for backpacking in the United States—in the national forest wilderness system.

Here comes another technicality that is very important. "Wilderness" is a federal designation of land set forth by the Wilderness Act of 1964. The act states that wilderness is "an area where the earth and its community of life are untrammeled by man, where man himself is a visitor who does not remain. … [Wilderness] is an area of undeveloped Federal land retaining its primeval character and influence, without permanent improvements or human habitation, which is protected and managed … to preserve its natural conditions. …[Wilderness] generally appears to have been affected … by the forces of nature, with the imprint of man's work substantially unnoticeable …. [It] has outstanding opportunities for solitude or a primitive and unconfined type of recreation, has at least five thousand acres of land or is of sufficient size as to make practicable its preservation and use in an unimpaired condition, and may also contain ecological, geological, or other features of scientific, educational, scenic, or historical value." Sounds perfect, right? It is—for a number of reasons. Wilderness differs markedly from the national forest land surrounding it. The way it works is that wilderness is inside of a national forest; the entire national forest is not designated as wilderness. If it's not wilderness, you can cut trees, mine the crap out of it, build dams, ski areas, and do all kinds of destructive things to it. Land that is designated specifically as wilderness is much more pristine—the crème de la crème of public land.

Of course there is no better or best wilderness area in the country. If it is designated as wilderness, then you can be pretty sure that there is something special there for you to explore. There are over 500 wildernesses to choose from, and my only advice is to look for places far away from urban areas or major highways. The more difficult it is to access and the farther away it is from an urban area, the less crowded and more pristine it will be—in most cases. And the bigger the better. To get more information on a specific wilderness area, or to explore other backpacking trails, go to *www.gorp.com* and click on "Wilderness Areas." This website is the best on earth for backpacking information. Another place to try for information is by calling National Forest and National Park headquarters. Odds are that they can help you out.

If you live in a state like, say, New York, and the amount of federally protected land is depressing (especially considering that the only nationally protected areas are national monuments that have nothing to do with outdoor recreation—e.g., Statue of Liberty National Monument), there is still hope. Check with the BLM, and your state park and state forest land stewards. Many state parks allow backpacking and are actually big enough to do it in. My experiences with state parks are limited, but most involve a short hike in to a campsite complete with concrete fire ring and picnic table—which is "ghetto," but still fun and always better than reality TV.

Still another option might be to look at a map and try to find a national recreation area or a national seashore. Sawtooth and Glen Canyon National Recreation Areas, for example, contain some of the best backpacking on earth. If you live close to the Canadian border, you should also investigate backpacking in their provincial and national parks, such as Banff and Jasper National Parks in Alberta where there are well over 1,000 miles of trails and scenery that put ours to shame.

esearch all of your possible options. You'll always be surprised at what you find. Besides, backpacking is about discovery, and I hope this section opens your eyes so that you can start exploring.

CHAPTER 4

USING A MAP

Oh yes, that terrible headache-provoking map. That indecipherable mumbo jumbo. That evil piece of paper with the squiggly-lined nonsense all over it. You shall learn how to use it! It actually takes a long time to really become a map-using machine. Not to discourage you, but it took me years to truly get it down. I'll give you some of the basics, and save the major stuff for Chapter 16. The following will help you find a map of the area you intend to backpack in, and figure out a good trail or trails for your trip.

There are several types of maps available for you to use for a backpacking trip. The most precise and always-available map is the U.S. Geological Survey (USGS) quadrangle map. They make one for each quad in the entire country. How convenient! These maps can be great when you need absolute precision, but on most occasions, you'll be much happier with something else. But if you can't find another version, you can always fall back on the quads. Another map that I'm familiar with is the national forest maps. Each national forest produces a general map of the entire national forest area. This is very much the opposite of the USGS quadrangle maps. These maps are not very specific or precise and cover a huge area. The biggest problem with these maps is that they, unlike the quadrangle maps, have no contour lines, which show elevation loss and gain. As a backpacker, these contour lines are essential to you. You will most certainly need a topographic map that has many of these intimidating contour lines, so forget about the general national forest maps. They are good for finding the trailhead and that's about it.

Some national forest districts do make specialized maps that differ from their general forest maps. These are quite a luxury, but you can't count on their availability. When they are available, these maps can be as good as any. They do tend, however, to be too imprecise, so watch out. Anything with a scale of over 1:100,000 is more or less useless. The ideal size is around half of that (1:50,000).

There are also dozens of independent map makers out there such as Latitude 40 Inc. and Earthwalk Press. My personal preference on backpacking maps is far and above, *National Geographic Trails Illustrated* maps (*http://maps.nationalgeographic.com/trails/*). Why? Because they are the perfect size, waterproof, topographic, and they focus on trails. In other words, the trails are brightly colored and stand out. They are easy to see when you're looking for where you're going. It's easy on the eyes, and almost every trail I've ever hiked appears on these maps—they are extremely thorough. They are also easy to order in advance and can also be downloaded fairly easily, although I'd still recommend purchasing a full-sized map printed on waterproof plastic paper. REI and other large outdoor stores now have map computers in their stores. You can locate a specific area, enlarge it to the size you want, and print exactly what you need on waterproof paper. The beauty of this is that you can get waterproof quadrangle maps that cover several quadrangles, allowing you to bring along only one quad map instead of three or four.

But you will always get more bang for your buck with a *Trails Illustrated* map. The only problem is that they don't make them for every backpacking area. Instead, they are made for areas that are particularly popular or good for backpacking. If there is a *Trails Illustrated* for the area you intend on exploring, then purchase it. They are the best option when they are an option. The maps also do a good job of marking streams—even the smallest ponds and lakes—tree-covered areas, barren areas, and other things that are very useful specifically for backpackers. Many other map-making companies make great maps for backpackers also. If there isn't a *Trails Illustrated*, then look into maps made by other companies. If you still can't find one, go with the USGS quadrangle maps. You may have to buy several of them, but they are extraordinarily precise and helpful. They can be purchased at national forest and parks offices and most backpacking stores, ordered from USGS offices nearby, or printed off of map computers in large outdoor stores such as REI.

Hopefully, now that I've sold you on the *Trails Illustrated* maps, you can find one for your area, and we can all talk about using maps and be on the same page. If not, at least make sure that whatever type of map you choose is topographic, highlights trails, color-codes forested and nonforested areas, and doesn't cover too much area (scale: 1:30,000–100,000). If a map fits this description, it is certainly suitable for gathering useful information.

Maps are incredible sources of information for us backpackers. They are the ultimate guide to trip planning. Looking at a map can excite me about an area, or deter me from going somewhere that I otherwise would have blindly walked into, not knowing what to expect. For example, I once took a trip to Telluride in hopes of doing some backpacking nearby. The mountains surrounding the small Colorado town are some of the most impressive in the lower 48. I figured I couldn't go wrong throwing a backpack on and heading out into them. Strangely, when I went into local outdoor store after local outdoor store, I couldn't find any *Trails Illustrated* maps of Telluride's backcountry. I found it odd and frustrating, but continued my search until I entered the last of the outdoor stores at the end of town.

I grabbed the last Telluride map that was wedged between the same Del Norte and Weminuche maps I had seen in every other store in town. Opening it up and taking a look, I realized that there was very little wilderness nearby. A small portion of land was circled with a wilderness boundary line—Mount Sneffels Wilderness—but inside the circle there were only a few miles of trail, and the rest was mostly slopes above treeline that were far too steep to hike. I also found something else very interesting. Scattered all over the area were small "x's" that I had never seen before. At first I had no idea what they were, but after scanning down the legend I noticed that the "x's" marked mines. The area was completely covered with these things. Why is that so bad? Seeing mines with yellow-stained rock every mile and strange cloudy water that you have no choice but to drink isn't my idea of a great trip. I put the map back on the shelf where it belonged and ended up going south to the Weminuche Wilderness (Colorado's largest at nearly a half million acres), and had a cleaner, quieter, and less crowded trip than I could have possibly found in Telluride.

Telluride is a great town and seemed promising for a good place to backpack, but I made the mistake of not directly seeking out a certain wilderness area. Everything wound up being just fine, because I got a good look at some maps and was able to bail on Plan A and make a different decision. So how can you pick a place, and what do you need to look for on your map to make a decision?

DECIDE DISTANCE FIRST

Figure out how long you're going to be out, what kind of hikers you and your companions are, and what kind of trip you're looking for. Do you want to cover a lot of miles and really get some exercise? Or are you gearing your trip towards a lot of campsite reading, fishing, and other things? The most ambitious hikers on earth can handle more than 30 miles a day. Some people have a hell of a time with 3. The average trip, I'd guess, would be 8–10 miles a day, so unless you feel like you are in exceptional physical condition, doing more than that may be exhausting. I've done trips where I covered 15–20 miles a day, and I've done trips where I covered 2 miles a day. I've also had trips where I wanted to cover large distances, and due to the terrain, I couldn't pull it off. You never know if you'll be able to cover the distances you set out to cover, so think small, especially if you're a beginner.

Also take your feet into consideration. If the skin on your feet is thicker than the leather on your boots, then they should be able to handle long distances, but if you get a pedicure every Thursday afternoon, and your feet get sore on about the 12th hole of your Saturday golf game, don't push them. Blisters, bruises, and who knows what else will turn your trip into a disaster, and you may never venture beyond the golf course again.

ADJUST FOR ALTITUDE

Look at the scale of your map and pay attention to the elevation contour lines. With most maps, each curvy line is equal to 40 feet in elevation. That means you are going 40 feet higher or lower in elevation with every line that you cross. Some maps use 80-foot lines, so the elevation gain per line is double. Still others increase and decrease in meters. Regardless of what the scale is, if the contour lines across the trail you're considering are as close together as a bar code, you might adjust the estimate of how far you'll be able to walk in one day. If you're out of shape and looking for a relaxing adventure, you might want to choose a different trail altogether—where contour lines are spread widely apart. I really like to mix up my trips between steep and flat, hard, and easy, and short and long, as much as possible because backpacking can be so many different things—spiritually cleansing, mentally focusing, and physically exhilarating. The difficulty of the terrain you choose can sometimes play a large role in the type of experience you will have.

WATER'S GOOD

Water, and making sure you'll have plenty, is the most important part of trip planning. I haven't mentioned it yet because most places have adequate water supplies. In most mountainous areas there are streams, lakes, rivers, and small ponds scattered all over, and there are usually tons of small trickling creeks and springs in between that don't show up on the map. That's not to say that you should take that for granted in the area you're planning on hiking. Always look to make sure there are plenty of blue lines and circles. If there is any doubt, contact the local Forest Service, National Park Service, state park service, or BLM office to make sure. If you are desert camping, you will have to plan your route carefully, or be prepared to carry all the water you need.

FIND A CAMPSITE

You probably won't be able to pinpoint the exact location of your campsites from looking at a map, but you will be able to tell if there are potential campsites in the area. The best campsites are near water, on level ground, and below timberline (if that's an issue where you are). In many places, campsites near water are hard to find. In other areas there are no trees and you will be forced to camp in a site more exposed to wind and lightning. But a map will tell you all that you need to know. Many maps, *Trails Illustrated* included, color-code areas that are tree-covered. If there is sufficient tree cover, the map will be tinted light green, while the surrounding terrain that is exposed or above tree line is in white. This helps to find ideal campsites. Maps show you where nice flat ground is, too. If you find a spot with no contour lines, or very few of them, it might be a great spot to camp. There is a chance that the ground will be marshy and wet, but heading to higher ground nearby usually solves that problem. At the very least, examining tree cover, water sources, and topography of a possible camping area will give you an idea of what to expect.

Sometimes a map can't answer your questions when it comes to campsites. In many backpacking areas, especially national parks, there are huge crowds that have forced the local land stewards to come up with a designated-campsite system. This means that you can camp only in campsites that are marked, and these marked sites won't show up on your map. The only way to find out about these is to obtain information from the National Park or National Forest Service office, or to pay careful attention to the information at the trailhead. Trailhead signboards usually contain info about designated sites and any other special camping regulations in the area. *Trails Illustrated* maps also sometimes point out which areas have designated sites, where camping is prohibited, where fires are not allowed, etc. This also helps to give you an idea of how difficult it will be to plan your campsites in advance.

Finally, in the busiest, most ridiculously chaotic backpacking spots in the country, you will need a backcountry permit. For national parks you must go to a national park backcountry office, usually located near a National Park Service headquarters or visitor center. For national forests, you must pay a visit to a Forest Service ranger station nearby. At either of these places, you will sign up for a trip and plan each day carefully. Only a certain number of people are allowed to camp in a certain area each night. Sure, your trip will be well planned, but you won't have much freedom to alter your plans if anything comes up—e.g., you really like a place and want to stay an extra day, or the hike was easier and shorter than you expected and you want to make it a little further. They say that changes of plans aren't that big of a deal, but it's just weird to feel like you're on some kind of schedule. Isn't that what you're trying to get away from? What a great system. I love that I get to pay to jump through those hoops too. Your best option—go somewhere else.

SOMEWHERE ELSE

I don't know what the future will bring for backpacking crowds, permits, and all that goes along with it, but I know what I do to avoid the herds. If you just happen to like backpacking in crowded areas then you are truly blessed,

I think. Personally, seeing hundreds of obnoxious, destructive people really turns me off. I don't like seeing barren, demolished campsites, giant fire pits, branchless trees, dead trees, human feces, dog feces, horse feces, toilet paper, trash, cigarette butts, barren stream banks, road-width trails, and certainly not trees with "Jim-Bob wuz here" carved into them. I'd rather just go somewhere else.

Some good trip planning and a map can help you avoid this crap nine times out of ten. First of all, to avoid the hordes of day-hikers and sightseers, pick a trail that is as far away from an urban area as possible. The bigger the urban area, the bigger the crowds will be at its surrounding natural areas. Hiking within an hour of large cities like Denver and Phoenix can be pretty nutty. It doesn't take a big city to produce huge crowds on accessible trails, though. Even in Aspen, a town of 5,000, trails within an hour's drive get over 100 people per day, while trails 90 minutes away get less than 100 people per year.

Another factor in escaping the crowds is to choose a trail that is hard to access. If the road to get there is gravel, it instantly cuts the number of visitors back by about half, it seems. If the road is long, windy, rocky, muddy, and generally ass-numbing as you bump along for a half hour or more, then odds are the trail won't be overrun with people—but I've seen exceptions. I think it works this way because crowded areas eventually get paved to accommodate all the traffic. So remember, if the road to get there is paved, be ready for a different kind of backpacking experience—one with little peace and quiet, torn up scenery, trash, and who knows what else. The key factor, still, is avoiding trails less than an hour or two away from a decent-sized town or city.

SELECTIVE SCENERY

Getting an idea of the scenery of an area, believe it or not, is also possible from looking at a topographic map. I don't want to proclaim that any one type of scenery is superior to any other, but I have on many occasions chosen a trail that climbed above tree line and was near rugged peaks instead of a different trail that was going to keep me in the trees the whole time. Once again, you can tell this on a map if it's color-coded, or if you just happen to know what elevation the trees cease to grow. With color-coded maps you can also tell where large meadows are, which are a great break in the scenery of a thick forest and have a unique feel of their own—sometimes superior to those mountain vistas. Anyway, I'm not going to carry on about this because if you're backpacking, you'll get scenery. You don't need a map to tell you that.

Really take a good look at maps and decipher as much information from them as possible. The tips I've given you are just some general things that can be determined. Study them hard and your trip will benefit from it. It will also help to familiarize you with the area, leading you towards not only a safer trip, but sparking your curiosities about the surrounding areas for future adventures. At the very least, picking a trip all on your own will give you a sense of discovery and accomplishment. Following a guidebook's recommendation will leave you feeling like another sheep in the herd. It will also give you a higher expectation for your trip, which can only lead to disappointment. Take pride in being self-sufficient. It's just another great aspect of the experience.

PART III
GET PACKING

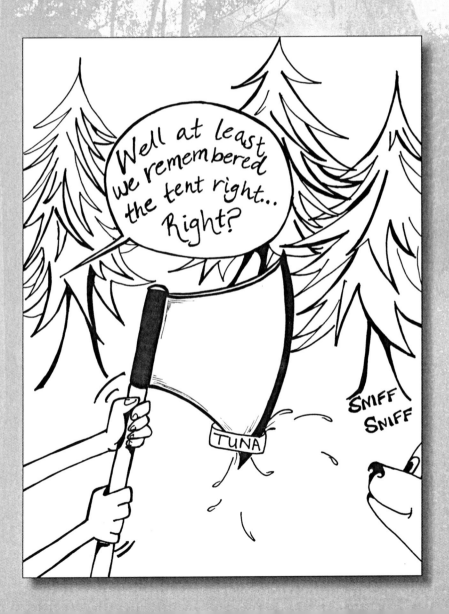

It was my first backpacking trip on duty as a

wilderness ranger.

It was Fourth of July weekend at Geneva Lake—just me and my supervisor, Todd. For food on the trip, I had brought a couple of Snickers and a loaf of bread—no more, no less. I didn't even know how to use a stove, and I'd never cooked anything for myself in my entire life. Besides, good food really didn't matter much to me. The excitement of the first overnighter with the Forest Service was enough to make the trip enjoyable, even if I was on the verge of overdosing on carbs by the time it was over.

"Hey Matt," my supervisor Todd said, "You can have some of my dinner. I've got extra."

"That's alright man, I'm fine. Thanks though."

"Listen, I can't bear to watch you sit there and eat more of that smashed bread. It's going to be good. Come help me."

"Okay, thanks Todd. Whatcha makin'?"

"Oh yeah, gonna fire it up, Lipton noodles with a little somethin' extra. Lil' bit a tuna baby."

"Ah hah, sounds pretty good."

"Yeah, these little noodle packages are pretty good, you just gotta add some extra stuff to make it really good … oh shit, I forgot, oh no!"

"What, what?"

"I forgot to bring a can opener."

"I wonder if we can pry it open with an ax. Here, give it to me." I grabbed the tuna can and slipped my hand down the handle of the ax until it was wedged just under the head. I pulled the bottom corner of the blade back and swung it downwards. *Thunk*. Nothing happened. I pulled it back a little farther and swung it again. *Thunk*. Only a small dent. On the third try I pulled the blade way back, and with a small thud the ax blade pierced the can. Tuna juice splattered all over my face, my shirt, in my hair, my eyes, on my bare leg.

"Dude, gross."

Todd laughed his usual hyena laugh as he rocked backwards on a small hill above me where he sat. I wiped the juice off the best I could and continued whacking away at the can, furthering the tuna juice splattering, but finally accomplishing the horrendous mission I set out to do from the beginning. Next time, I hoped he'd remember his can opener, because it was definitely going to be his turn to open the tuna.

The list of things I've forgotten over the years is quite long—some more important than others. The list includes rain jacket (and it rained), flashlight (and I didn't make it back to camp before dark), map (and I got lost), compass (and I couldn't find my way back), toilet paper (and I couldn't hold it), pocket knife (and my tent pole broke and I couldn't fix it—oh yes, and it rained all night), and many other important and not-so-important items. The things you forget are annoying at best, but some things can be of life-and-death importance. I'm still alive, so I found a way to get by, but if the weather had been worse, or I had gotten lost in an area that I was less familiar with, I could have been in much more serious trouble.

The most frightening situation I've had was the time I forgot my headlamp. I was camped a few miles down the trail and got into a big conversation with a trail volunteer that I was working with. By the time we were finished, sunset had fallen, and I had three miles to go to get back to camp. After two miles of jogging and speed-walking down the hill, it was completely dark. Completely. I couldn't even see the trail well enough to keep from tripping and stumbling my way along. It was raining hard and my body was quivering under my rain gear. Eventually, after another exhausting hour of feeling my way through the forest—my arms stretched out to shield my face and body from branches and even whole trees—I finally found my tent. Another hour of that, and hypothermia could have easily set in.

Organization and preparation could have prevented almost all of these mistakes. I rarely forget or misplace items anymore, because I've come up with a good organized system for myself. It works well for me, and some of the advice I'll give you in the following chapters should help you too.

The greatest thing about being organized and prepared is that it is easy to motivate for a trip. Packing takes less time, you don't forget much, and in general you'll be more inclined to go. After all, packing and organizing your gear is probably the greatest deterrent to going backpacking. It's the not-fun part that everyone has to suck up and do before the adventures can begin. Get organized and stay organized, and more adventures will come—adventures seeing great mountains, peaceful forests, glimmering lakes and streams, and all the things our earth has to offer—not adventures with eating food by hand, stumbling in the dark, opening cans with axes or rocks, or battling with hypothermia after forgetting your raincoat.

CHAPTER 5

GETTING ORGANIZED

"**G**et organized." What a repetitive cliché of a phrase that is. You've heard it from your mom, your teachers, your boss, and now me. For most of us it's a pretty painful thing to do, but Mom and your teachers were right. Getting organized is a valuable thing. Unfortunately, no one ever really tells you how to get organized, nor do they tell you what that really means. They just tell you to do it, and you have to figure it out for yourself. I didn't have much help either, but I did solve a few mysteries. This chapter will throw out some useful tips. Hopefully some will work for you, and maybe, just maybe, you'll actually put in the time and effort it takes to get organized. It's really not too tough. Hey man, if I can do it. . . .

GEAR

The big stuff is usually easy to keep track of. Let's face it, it's easier to lose a blister kit than it is to lose your sleeping bag. The good news is that the most important stuff is the gear that is big and hard to lose. It's so big and important that it's hard to ever forget, and I admit that I've never forgotten my backpack, my sleeping bag, my sleeping pad, or my tent. These four items comprise your "big items" list, and can be kept wherever you can find room for them—closet, storage unit, etc.

BIG THINGS
- Backpack
- Sleeping bag
- Tent
- Sleeping pad

Then it gets more difficult. The remaining things I like to keep in one box in one place. Splitting it into two boxes might even be better, but one is fine. In this box will be all your small and medium-sized backpacking gear. The most important thing you can do is to make sure that everything down to the tiniest detail is in that box—and see that it all gets back in that box when you return from your trip. It's also a good idea to inventory everything as you put it in the box to develop a personal checklist. Yes, this is a bit nerdy, and I don't have my own little checklist, but I've also backpacked a couple of hundred times and don't need one anymore. But I find that keeping everything in one place is just as effective. The biggest problem I have is remembering the things I use regularly when I'm not backpacking—such as clothes, raincoat, toothbrush, etc. These items can't live in the box if I use them every day. If you are able to have a separate backpacking set of everything, then do so. If not, just try your best to remember, or maybe even make a list of things you will need that don't live in the box. Enough of that, let's see what's in the box.

MEDIUM-SIZED THINGS
- Raingear
- Water filter
- Water bottles
- Warm clothes + hat and gloves
- Other clothing (socks, T-shirts, hat, etc.)
- First-aid kit
- Flashlight/headlamp
- Toilet paper
- Poop shovel
- Plastic bags/extra stuff sacks
- Cooking pot/frying pan
- Stove
- Fuel
- Nonperishable food items (see page 70)

SMALL THINGS
- Sunglasses
- Sunscreen
- Lighter and/or matches
- Maps
- Compass
- Watch
- Medication(s)
- Pocketknife or Leatherman

- Toothbrush
- Toothpaste
- Floss
- Other toiletries
- Fingernail clippers (for long trips)
- Rope or twine
- Potholder
- Pot scrubber
- Plastic eating utensils
- Dish soap

This list is fairly solid, but there may be several items that you want to bring that aren't there, for example, a camera, a journal, a book, fishing equipment, etc. I just want to make sure that there aren't too many things on the list—only the basics with a few common useful items to go with it. And remember, many items on these lists are far from essential. The cooking equipment certainly isn't required. Some trips, I bring the full kitchen arsenal, and sometimes I bring food that can be eaten without cooking, which saves time and weight, especially on shorter trips. Besides, you could bring just a pot and cook over a wood fire if it is permitted where you are going. Who needs a stove and fuel? No one, but they can really come in handy, and I would surely miss them on a long trip.

The point is, as I've said 63 times already, is to leave whatever you can at home. If you can think of an alternative to carrying it and using it, then give it a shot. Essential items are essential items, but at least half the stuff you bring with you isn't really necessary. The more optional items you can get used to living without the better off you'll be. Light loads and small backpacks make for happy faces. Hold on, let's pause for a minute to enjoy that remarkably dreamy sentence I just created. Wow, it sounds so bright and cheerful I feel like running out and buying some fabric softener and a Happy Meal. Paint me up like a clown, and I could give Ronald a run for his McNugget.

FOOD

Anyways, back to getting organized. As you may have noticed, one of the items I threw into your list was nonperishable food items. This is a great organizing trick. It may sound like a really anal thing to do, and it probably is, but it is a real time-saver on packing. Storing all of your equipment in one place will certainly save you much time and hassle, but keeping a good supply of food that you like to eat while backpacking can save even more. What am I talking about?

Well, think about what you often eat while backpacking. If you've never backpacked, try to envision something that might be easy on the trail. I keep an actual separate food box, dedicated to food and cooking equipment. In the box are my stove, pots and pans, utensils, and fuel, as well as a number of items that I commonly take with me. These things all live happily in my food box: oatmeal, Cream of Wheat, fast-cooking pasta, instant rice, instant beans, dehydrated food, powdered milk, sugar, baking powder, flour, etc. Instead of going through my cabinets for all kinds of things, I keep it all right there—ready for action.

Before a trip I'll throw a couple of handfuls of oats into a plastic bag, toss in some raisins, some cinnamon, brown sugar, and powdered milk. Add water and heat it up at camp and it's done. Breakfast is covered and ready to go in the backpack in less than a minute. For dinner I might scoop out some rice and some instant refried beans into separate baggies. For another dinner I might fill a bag with orzo (it's a type of pasta, Emeril) and throw in some sun-dried tomatoes, garlic powder, dried herbs, and salt and pepper. Again, at camp I boil it for a few minutes and dinner is served. How long did I spend searching for ingredients and packing them into a plastic bag? A whole minute.

If you have all of those ingredients in your box, you can do that. Figure out what you like, what goes in it, what won't go bad, and keep it in the box. You can even keep a stash of plastic bags ready to go. A little preparation in this category goes a long way. We'll get into this in much more detail in Chapter 11. Even if you just keep a huge supply of oatmeal, mac 'n' cheese, and ramen noodles in there, you'll still be saving time and energy in the food-packing department. A huge shopping trip before you go backpacking can be quite an ordeal. It's kept me from going on a short two- or three-day excursion more times than I'd like to admit. Do try this food-box thing at home. Don't pretend you're too cool or too busy to do it, either. I've done enough pretending in those two categories for the both of us.

CHAPTER 6

PACK THE PACK

No, we didn't just talk about this. We talked about getting organized. Now we're going to discuss how to pack all that stuff. No, I don't think you're an idiot, but there are a few things I want to point out. It's all about physics, man, and when I say "physics," I'm not talking about the people that can see the future. How you pack your bag can and does make a difference. There are certain techniques that people prefer, but the general ideas are pretty much agreed upon.

First of all, put your heaviest stuff on the bottom and as close to your back as possible. Most backpacks are designed to carry your sleeping bag at the very bottom, which doesn't make a whole lot of sense to me, but then again, a lot of things don't make much sense to me—like why so many food corporations feel that artificial color makes food look appetizing and not toxic and frightening. Okay, so your sleeping bag will probably be at the very bottom, but next up should be your food. Food, unless you have a rice cake addiction, is always going to be pretty dense and heavy. The other dense items that you want close to your body are your stove, pots and pans, water filter, and fuel.

Having the dense, dead-weight stuff close to your body makes the load less awkward and heavy. Picture carrying a 10-foot-long log. Is it easier to hold in the center with the log pressed up against your chest, or is it easier to hold it on one end while the other is 10 feet in front of you? Odds are you couldn't keep the opposite end of the log off the ground if you were holding onto one end with both hands. Physics man. Crazy. The same is true with your load of stuff. You don't want your heaviest items dangling on the outside. The weight will pull your shoulder straps back, putting more pressure on your chest, shoulders, and the front of your armpits. This gets bad after several hours. Trust me. I've spent months of my life carrying loads in a way that makes less sense than splicing fish genes into a plant. Backpack manufacturers have even gone so far as to come up with all kinds of compression systems that specifically suck your pack closer into your body in one tight little package.

The biggest problem, I think, is where to pack your tent. So many times I've carried my tent on the outside of my pack, completely ruining any strategy that I was trying on the inside. I think the trick here is to remove the tent poles and stakes and always keep them separate. Backpacks will often have straps on the sides that accommodate these well. I'd recommend putting poles on the side, still as close to you as possible, and stuff the rest of the tent that otherwise wouldn't have fit into your pack on the inside.

To further secure your heaviest items, pack your clothing all around them like you're trying to protect a fragile wedding gift. After that, throw in other miscellaneous items, still trying to pack them as close to your body as possible. The only thing left to consider now is where to put stuff that you will be using frequently and don't want to have to dig around for every hour. Here comes another problem. Water. Water is, as you hopefully have discovered at some point in your life, very heavy. Each quart is two pounds, which in backpacking terms is enormous. It is also probably the most dense object you are carrying. Try your very best to keep these close to your body in a place that is also accessible. Most packs have good side pouches for water bottles. These aren't ideal, but it beats having them slosh and shift around on the very top of your backpack—away from body. Another option is to use a water pouch, manufactured by CamelBak, REI, and other outfitters. Unfortunately for me, sucking water out of a tube is akin to hearing fingernails being scraped across a chalkboard, and I don't like using them. If I did, the rest of my body would surely benefit from it. Most backpacks now have slots available right between your shoulder blades to put these CamelBak pouches. Buying one of these could really pay off if you plan to backpack regularly, which you should, because backpacking kicks ass.

Other items you want to be able to reach quickly are your raincoat, compass, map, sunscreen, sunglasses, and toilet paper (especially if you forgot the water filter). I usually keep all of these lightweight things in the top pouch of my backpack. Most packs have pouches on top that fold over the main compartment. They are great and are usually the perfect size to accommodate such items. If you don't have a happy little pouch on top, it's no big deal; put the light stuff wherever you want. The point is that you can put light items wherever you like. It's the heavy stuff that needs to be secured close to your body. Do this and it will make a 40-pound load feel like 30 instead of 50. Sounds good, huh?

The last bit of advice I can give on packing is to do it the night before. I rarely practice what I preach in this department, but hey, I'm workin' on it. I have slept in too late so many times or had to do something all morning, and by the time I was ready to start packing I doubted whether it would be worth the trouble. This is very much a mystery because I know damn well that it is always worth it, but the phenomenon of early-afternoon sluggishness has a way of permeating my brain and turning it into an irrational, cheeselike substance. If you too have this problem, then you really must get it in gear the night before and pack your bag. If not, you may never make it outdoors again. Even worse, you might choose to rent Ernest movies over going backpacking. Oh, c'mon, I never did that! That's just an example. I spend every waking hour of my life either backpacking or writing about backpacking. I know not the meaning of the word "lazy." Quick, end the chapter!

PART IV
DINING OUT

Greg and I

booked it up the trail the best we could.

We had to stop every five or ten minutes when the terrain had an uphill slant to it, but we were flying when we were on the move. Our dads weren't too far behind, but they were no match for us. I tried hard not to let Greg know what a struggle it was to carry that monstrous load on my back. It was a mere three-day trip, but we were all loaded up like pack animals on a two-week expedition for some reason. Unfortunately, none of us really knew any better.

We had made a brief stop for water earlier, but it was time for a real break. That meant food. I suppose our first snack on the trail was pretty tasty, but I can't imagine it being the most sensible snack for a bunch of out-of-shape flat-landers. "Well boys," my dad said, "ready to sit down and have a snack?" That idea went over well. All of us nodded or gave a "yep" as we wiggled out of our packs. "What do you boys want? We've got, let's see, apples, trail mix ..."

"Hey Dad, the Oreos are in my pack," I said, pulling out a nice big bag of unopened Oreos. I ripped open the plastic and immediately shortened one of the four black- and white-striped rows of cookies. I think I ate about 10 before we left that spot. The only intelligent thing I did was eat one of the apples that I had been carrying in a plastic sack. Yes, that's right, I was carrying a couple of pounds of apples by hand because the four of us, with gigantic packs, couldn't seem to find a place to put them—anywhere.

The trail was flat for a while, otherwise we might have added four piles of chocolaty Oreo sludge to the scenery. We held down the cookies just fine as we kept on going up the 12-mile trail that we had planned to tackle on our first day. You heard me, 12 miles. The afternoon clouds moved in like they always do and brought buckets of rain. Needless to say we all began looking around for a campsite at what we thought was about 9 miles in. It felt like 90 miles, but after returning to this trail a couple of years later, I discovered that we were about halfway up the trail and had climbed about 1,000 feet of the total 3,000-foot ascent. I sure didn't remember our hike as being slightly steeper than Kansas and only six little miles. I just remember it being a full day, and the pain of putting that pack back on two days later for the hike out.

The first night we had quite a dinner. Although we had carried apples and three pounds of Oreos and God knows what else up that trail, we somehow thought that a prepackaged backpacking meal would really hit the spot. We even brought a prepackaged, "just add water" dessert. Hey, they were dehy-drated backpacker meals, perfect right? So we tried the chili. Instead of us all saying "mmm" in unison as we dug into our pouches of chili, we all started laughing. "Wow, this is delicious huh guys?" my dad said as the four of us nearly choked. I think Greg laughed so hard that a mouthful of chili oozed out of his mouth back into the shiny aluminum pouch. So we sat by our campfire, giggling from time to time as a food-related comment arose, all the while shoving gob after gob of the "gruel" down our throats.

Then came our fabulous "just add water" dessert. Surely it would be better than our previous chili experience, we thought. Wrong again. The "German Chocolate Cheesecake" that was recommended highly by the woman at the outdoor store didn't impress us in the same way it had impressed her. We quickly added it to the list of food items that we called "gruel." I don't think we even had the courage to finish that one, and it was a dessert. How do you screw up dessert?

We survived through our first full meal, and although it was nothing short of terrible, the laughs we shared made it one of the most memorable meals of my life. Breakfast the next morning was totally different. Everybody's favorite, that's right, Spam, and home fries fried up in a big 12-inch skillet, yum. Spam was actually quite a treat compared to the gruel from the night before. I think my dad almost forgot about carrying five pounds of potatoes for a moment— almost. Greg's dad almost forgot about carrying that giant frying pan, leaving no room for the sack of apples that I had to carry in my ice-cold hand as rain pelted me all afternoon. For 15 minutes, we almost forgot, but I remember carrying that pack much more than my plate full of Spam and fried potatoes with only a little salt and pepper sprinkled on them.

I don't quite recall what we had for lunch, but I think we had something along the lines of a peanut butter and jelly sandwich. You know, something that requires packing multiple glass jars full of heaviness. Not only do you get to carry those heavy glass jars up the mountain, you get to carry them back down too! Oh boy! Even if you eat peanut butter and jelly until you're ready to vomit, you still have to lug the jars back down the mountain. The bread was excellent also. After being constricted in a backpack for hours the day before, each slice took on a whole new shape. Somehow I remembered the loaf being big, fluffy, and soft. I was proven wrong once again as we ate little crumbly pieces of smashed, deformed bread.

Dinner that night was actually not too bad, but not something anyone can count on. Fortunately, as a group, our fishing skills far exceeded our backpacking skills, and we managed to capture a few unlucky trout from the nearby stream. Fresh, stream-caught, wild trout are one of the most delicious things on earth. It accompanied our ramen noodles well, and weight-wise, you can't get much better. After another Oreo binge for dessert, it was decided that we could all handle having three-course meals like this every time. I don't remember what we had for breakfast the next day, our last meal of the trip, but I remember having several choices from our giant pile of leftover food. We still hauled out a good 20 pounds of food and trash from that two-night trip, but our packs really did lighten up. That just goes to show how much we actually brought.

So how did the story end? After returning back to civilization, Greg's dad's knee was swollen and stiff from carrying too much weight. He hung out around the house until it was time for him to fly home. When he did get up, he limped around like a 6'-5" Igor. For weeks my dad and I complained about bringing too much stuff, and he felt partly responsible for the knee injury. After all, it was my dad that was making most of these poor decisions for us, but I don't recall anyone trying to stop him from buying one of everything in the camping store. We learned some lessons on that trip, but we still really didn't know what to do for the next one. I don't think Greg or his dad have been backpacking since then. That was nine summers ago. My dad has only been a handful of times. I guess I was the only one meant to truly overcome the obstacles. The obstacles of having your mind and body associate "backpacking" with "huge drawn-out, painful, strenuous ordeal."

I f I've learned anything since my first trip, it's that backcountry food can be simple, light, and easy to organize, and it's the area that can really make or break a good backpacking adventure. It can help make any trip outstanding, and the most weight is saved from packing certain foods and leaving others at home. I honestly believe that the flavor and quality of your food doesn't have to be compromised either. When it's done right, organizing food for a trip isn't an overwhelming ordeal at all. Getting your food together easily and eating good meals at the campsite makes any adventure more enjoyable. The goal of this section is not to tell you how to do it, because every human being is different. We like different foods, different clothes, and different places. Some like to cook, others don't. Some love the flavor of MSG-saturated packaged foods, and some people eat only organic. Others can't go 24 hours without a huge slab of red meat, while others won't eat honey because it comes from innocent little exploited bees.

The focus is more towards leading a beginner or even an experienced backcountry cook in the right direction. To truly become an expert, you must think about the suggestions I make. Think about the foods you like and how you make some of your favorite dishes at home. Think about any backpacking experiences you've had in the past and how my suggestions relate to something stupid that you've done. This section is written to inspire you to look at foods at the grocery store a little differently. It's written to make you organize your backpacking food in ways you never thought of before. Ultimately, it's written to make backpacking more enjoyable and easy than it's ever been.

Whether you're a chef or you depend on Chef Boyardee, take charge of your food, and it will enhance all your backpacking experiences. The best backcountry meals are simply and quickly prepared, easy to pack, easy to carry, and good sources of energy for the trail—but that doesn't mean they can't be good. Even though they are simple, your wilderness meals should be some of the best of your life. The setting is perfect, your hungry stomach makes food taste even better, and you're usually sharing your food with one of the most important people in your life—your relatives, your best friends, your honey buns, or even a drooling four-legged friend. Do yourself a favor and make sure that bad or heavy food never steals that pleasure.

CHAPTER 7

CHEF BOYARDEE

Hey, if you depend on this fat "mofo" for survival, that's okay. There's nothing wrong with not knowing how to cook your own food—except that you end up not knowing what's in your food. Some highly commercialized food products contain ingredients that are still mysterious to modern science. Anyway, I have no disrespect for you noncooks, other than I think you are all sick in the head. Okay, okay, dehydrating food, for the vast majority of the general public, is not a fun hobby. Personally, I'm not a big fan of the fine art of crocheting or doll making, so I can relate. So for you, Mr. or Ms. shortcut, here are the quick solutions to all your outdoor cooking needs.

BREAKFAST FOODS

This shouldn't change much from what you eat at home—unless you are a pizza-and-beer-for-breakfast person. Warm cereals and grains are the best. Oatmeal, grits, Cream of Wheat. What more could you ask for. You can also bust out the Froot Loops. Eat them plain or bring some powdered milk, and yes, your hesitation about powdered milk is pretty much right on. There ain't no way that stuff is going to taste the same as milk from a carton, but it's better than nothing and a great source of protein and all that. Speaking of powdered milk, I would highly recommend adding it to almost all of your breakfast foods. Also experiment with soy milk powder. Give those cows' infected, steroid-pumped nipples a break. I think it tastes better myself, but I'm also a stinky hippie, which allows me to enjoy a vast array of foods that others find dirtlike in flavor.

Slightly more complicated but tastier breakfasts might include pancakes with dried blueberries, yogurt and Granola (only for the first day or two), salsa, beans, and tortillas, and even ham and eggs if you don't mind the extra weight.

LUNCH FOODS

Lunch, on short trips, is the easiest meal to put together, but on long trips it can be very difficult. For short trips I like to get a lot of snacky foods for lunch—cheese and crackers, cheese and bread, bagels, nuts, Granola bars, dried fruit, and trail mixes. It's also easy to bring luncheon meats, which will almost always keep for two full days. Sometimes peanut butter and jelly sandwiches can be really nice, but use bagels or some other nonsquishable bread. Also make sure that you're not bringing giant jars of peanut butter and jelly—just bring what you need or even make the sandwiches ahead of time.

Long trips, like I said, can complicate lunches—especially for someone looking for a quick and easy fix for food. For most lunches, you will be on the go, and you won't want to stop and cook anything. Bagels, bread, cheese, and luncheon meats that you once depended on are now moldy and stale. What can you eat? The key to good lunches on a long trip is to save leftovers from dinner. Make some extra rice and beans, wrap them up in a tortilla, and throw them in a sealable plastic container. Turn last night's pasta into today's pasta salad. Maybe even try mac 'n' cheese cold. You get the idea.

DINNER

This should be easy. You'll most likely be eating your normal staples: mac 'n' cheese, ramen noodles, prepackaged rice and pasta meals. Also look into buying dehydrated meals—the ones that come in a silver pouch, and instant products made by Fantastic Foods. Also for a few quick and easy calories, I love to bring dehydrated cups of soup. All you have to do is boil a little extra water and you're good to go. If you get sick of these and want to venture out into the world of wilderness culinary arts, read the following chapters. Give it a try. You might surprise yourself.

CHAPTER 8

DEHYDRATED FOOD

Dehydrated food is not as bland as you might expect. In fact, some foods can be dehydrated and brought back to life very well. Not everyone owns a dehydrator, but I would recommend buying one if you plan to do a substantial amount of backpacking before the day you die. I use mine only a few times a year, but in only a few years it will have paid off. I will have saved a little money by doing it myself, eaten better food than the prepackaged just-add-water stuff, and saved myself from carrying hundreds of pounds. If you insist that dehydrating your own food is too much of a hassle, there are still options for you.

First of all, if you happen to have an oven you can get by without a dehydrator. Place whatever you want to dehydrate on sheet pans or oven racks and close the door. If it's a gas oven with a pilot light, the heat given off by the pilot light should be enough to do the trick. If not, turn it to low and rotate occasionally until crispy dry—or close to it. The same goes for electric ovens. Convection ovens are prime for dehydrating, perhaps even better than a good old-fashioned dehydrator itself—and a lot bigger. The pilot light only with the fan on is ideal.

If you still refuse to give it a chance, there are several dehydrated products commonly found in grocery stores. Melissa's is a brand that specializes in exotic, high-quality dried foods. They make currants, morel mushrooms, lobster mushrooms, and chipotles, just to name a few. Most of the stuff I have tried is pretty good, but you will find out quickly that dehydrating your own food is the most economical alternative. Plus it's fun, alright? I swear.

Cheaper stuff that is commonly found and quite tasty is sun-dried tomatoes, instant beans, all kinds of dried fruit, jerky, and herbs. All of these I prefer to buy instead of do myself. None of the above, especially fruit and herbs, are cheaper to dry at home, and there is always a great selection at any store. Raisins, "craisins," and sun-dried cherries, currants, and apricots are really good and pretty cheap, with the exception of the cherries. The only fruit I ever do at home is pineapple because the stuff at the store is always too sweet for me. Basil, oregano, thyme, cilantro, marjoram, dill, and others can be found at any supermarket. Even though dried herbs are a pretty weak substitute for fresh ones, they do add some flavor, which may interest you unless you happened to have lost your tongue in a nasty stamp-licking accident.

If you have a dehydrator, congratulations. They are fun to use and play around with. It's always interesting to find out how something will turn out, and how it will rehydrate later at the campsite. The first thing I ever dehydrated was zucchini. I made little chips out of them that were "dee-lish." I don't think I ever got the chance to rehydrate any of them because I snacked on them right out of the bag. There are times when dehydrating sounds like a painful chore, but when I actually get motivated to spend a few bucks at the store and a half hour of my time, it is always easy and pays off huge in the summer months.

From all my experiments, I must say, some foods dehydrate well, and some don't. There are also fun ways to try and add flavor to dried meat and produce. For example, try grilling, roasting, or marinating vegetables and meats before you dehydrate them. Just don't use oil or your foods won't dehydrate as well. Here are some of my favorites:

- zucchini, squash, and eggplant
- roasted peppers
- asparagus
- broccoli and cauliflower
- mushrooms
- spinach
- red meats
- green onions
- corn
- peas
- mango
- pineapple

The possibilities go on from here. Most importantly, dehydrating food gives you the ability to add variety to your diet. Variety, in many ways, can be the key to good nutrition, and good nutrition is the key to a healthy backpacking trip. Your food won't actually be as tasty on the trail as it is at home, but if you take the time and effort to prepare your own food, it will taste even better to your biased tongue. Pound for pound, dehydrated food is the best trail food you can bring. It is weightless and doesn't take up too much space. It makes camp cooking more fun, more nutritious, and more delicious than wimping out and buying prepackaged stuff at the store. If you are intimidated by dehydrating your own food, don't be. Dehydrators are very affordable and easy to use, and you may be able to dry food in your own oven or even outside in the sun. Hell,

Grizzly Adams, you can just smoke everything over an open fire in your back yard. That'll fix yer wagon, Pa.

Dehydrating can still be a drag sometimes if you're trying to prepare for a trip in the near future. The key to making it a reasonable task is timing. The worst thing you can possibly do is wait until a few days before your backpacking trip to get ready. If packing up seems like a monumental task that must be started several days before the trip, it becomes less enjoyable. At least that's how I see it. Dehydrating food, for the most part, should be done at a time that's most convenient, not only to you, but to your wallet if you load up when produce is cheap and in-season. I suppose most people enjoy waiting until the last moment to get things done, but getting a little done here and there is much less painful for me. Dehydrating is a great way to store extra food, especially if your freezer is already full of ancient soups and unidentified objects like mine is.

The most exciting aspect of dehydrating food is the ability to dehydrate liquids. Most dehydrators come with plastic sheets for making fruit rolls. Basically, you puree fruit, pour it on the sheet, and you've got your own fruit rolls. It's tougher than buying store-bought rolls, but easier to digest without the high-fructose corn syrup, artificial color, and who knows what else. The excitement comes along when you start dehydrating homemade salsa, pasta sauce, and others. Dehydrated marinara can be brought back to life so well at camp it should be outlawed.

Finally, it should be noted that storing dried food in the refrigerator or freezer can add life to it. If you leave it out at room temperature, it will last for a long time. There's no doubt about that, but it never hurts to keep things cool. It should extend the shelf life by at least double, and it'll just plain taste better. Have I made my point yet? Can we keep moving along here people?

CHAPTER 9

BRINGING PERISHABLES

Bringing perishable can be tricky. For the most part, I don't recommend doing it, but there are some perishables that you can bring that will survive for the better part of a week. They work great for short trips, but they can be eaten on the first few days on a long trip, too. Some perishables last a very long time, especially drier cheeses such as parmesan. These are excellent items to have with you. Bringing in T-bones, on the other hand, might not be such a bright idea. If you are a meat lover, there are several options other than jerky. If you love cream cheese on your bagels, it takes a while for it to get sour, and if you can find some sealed cream cheese packets, threaten nearby customers, push them out of the way, do whatever you need to do to grab a hand/pocketful. There's plenty of hydrated things to choose from.

MEATS

Although I usually go the "fresh caught trout" route, I do know of some tasty and easy meats to bring into the backcountry. Yes, I said "bring"—let those deer fatten up for winter in peace. For example:

- Smoked salmon or lox (last for several days)
- Luncheon meats (only last for the first two days at the most)
- Jerky (lasts so long it's scary)
- Canned meat (too heavy, but tuna can be good on occasion)
- Bacon (doesn't last long raw, but if you cook it until it's nice and crispy before you leave, you'll have some nice bacon bits to munch on for several days—bacon goes well with soups, pasta, chili, and many other dishes)
- Marinated raw meats (good for one-night trips—marinades with salt, oil,

vinegar, and sugar help to preserve the meat a little longer and keep bacteria from brewing)

- Eggs (they can go unrefrigerated for a while, but always fully cook them to make sure; some nifty plastic egg containers are sold at most camping stores)
- Summer sausage (bulky, but a tasty snack and a great source of protein to accompany any meal, and it lasts for a long time)
- Spam (if you dare!)

CHEESES

A hunk of cheese can be the best snack on a backpacking trip. Cheese is a good protein and fat source and keeps surprisingly well, especially drier cheeses. The less moisture in the cheese, the longer it takes to go bad—generally. Grated parmesan is a must for backcountry pastas, especially the real deal (parmigiano reggiano). I like to bring cheddar or jack for burritos and snacks to go with crackers and sandwiches. I usually start out my trips with some sliced swiss on a sandwich or two as well. I even put a little cream cheese in my backpack for bagels. I have no comment on Cheez Whiz.

FRUITS AND VEGETABLES

Fresh fruits and vegetables are delicious, but fragile and heavy. Many fruits and vegetables must be left at home. Sorry grapefruit, sorry mangoes, sorry tomatoes, sorry potatoes. Some fruits and vegetables are great to bring. Cherries are light, delicious, and cheap in the summer. Raspberries and blueberries can be good if you can keep them from getting demolished in your pack. Plums and kiwis are good too, but remember you'll have to pack out pits from the plums and skins from the kiwis. Vegetables are a little tougher to deal with. There aren't many light vegetables, but bringing them for the first night or on a one-night trip might work well. The only vegetables I typically bring are garlic and shallots, but garlic and onion powders are still lighter and easier.

CHAPTER 10

COOKING PARAPHERNALIA

Like everything in backpacking, it's good not to get carried away with cooking equipment. Cooking utensils, most of them, are a waste of space, time, and energy. It goes along with the "don't bring your whole house with you" rule. Bring as little as possible, and remember, more than half the people in the world eat with their hands. Plates, bowls, and cups can be a drag too. You have more stuff to wash and carry. I almost never bring any kind of plate or bowl with me because my hiking companions and I are always comfortable enough with each other to eat straight out of the pot or pan. If you must bring separate containers, make sure, as always, that you can use them for several different things; otherwise, it's not truly worthwhile to bring them. The same goes for pots and frying pans. Try to bring one or the other, and make do with only one stove.

Plates, bowls, and cups are best left at home if you have the courage. Nalgene water bottles, especially the transparent plastic ones, make great containers for hot drinks. Plates and bowls are one thing, but you should never bring cups. That's what water bottles are for. If you must bring separate containers for eating, bring a nice big round Tupperware. Use the lid for a plate, and the inside for a bowl. Use the container for whatever else you can. If you must bring it, you might as well use it. Store burritos in there, pasta salad, or bread that you don't want to get squished. At least pack your cooking supplies in there—your spices, salt and pepper, oil, forks, spoons, pocketknife, potholder, dish soap, and scouring pad. The more you fit in the Tupperware, the less net space it takes up in your pack. Nalgene also makes wonderful plastic containers designed for food. The lids screw on so they won't fly off in your pack and leave a nice pile of squished food all over your clothes.

Try to bring one of the following only: pot or frying pan. Bring neither if you can live off bagels and candy bars without any regret. Whatever you do, don't pack both and only bring one stove. If you are going with a group of four or more, all rules go out the door. It only makes sense to bring extra stuff if there are extra people to carry it. Otherwise, don't do it.

There are several other kitchen utensils you could bring, but I would not recommend it. Wooden spoons, spatulas, whisks, etc. can be left at home. These are all luxury items anyway. If you have a fork or spoon to eat with, then you can use it just the same as the fancier versions that you use at home. I would also recommend getting in the habit of cooking without using measuring cups and spoons. Trust your judgment. If the rice isn't cooked and there is no water left in the pot, add a little bit. If your oatmeal is so thick your wrist gets tired from stirring it, add a little more water. Adding too much water isn't a problem either. Add more cornmeal to your polenta or more potato dust to your watery instant mashed potatoes. You can also just let it simmer and wait for some of the water to evaporate if you have plenty of fuel and ten minutes to spare.

The key is making do with as little as possible. Although a wooden spoon and a measuring cup don't weigh much, it's the attitude that will get you in trouble. If you think it would be nice to have, you will think that about other things too. Your pack will be full of extra T-shirts, lanterns, books, oranges, food, batteries, blankets, beer, and deodorant. Pretty soon you've got a miserable 60 pounds on your back for a three-day trip, and the things you thought would make the trip more fun ended up making your feet hurt so bad you couldn't make it to that gorgeous lake at the end of the trail. Bring what you need to get by. Cooking utensils and equipment are no exception. If you want to go all out on food, do it in the form of preparation at home. The grocery baggers will even help you carry it from the store to your car.

FINDING A STOVE

I'd like to be able to tell you the ultimate stove to use, but the ultimate stove for one person may not be the ultimate stove for another. It depends on how you like to cook, where you like to cook, and what is most important to you. Some stoves use cheap, low-energy fuel and are refillable. Some stoves use expensive high-powered fuel with canisters that you throw away or recycle. Some stoves are put together and lit easily, but have problems in high winds and at high elevation. Some stoves are light and compact and cost a fortune, while some cost $25 and weigh a little more. There are too many stoves to possibly list them all, and they are constantly evolving. So, ignore price and shop around for the stove that best fits your style of backpacking. Are you going to use it on Everest or near calm lakes at 11,000 feet in the Sierra Nevadas? Also stick to top brands (MSR, Primus, Gaz, Coleman)—not only because they are better but because their specific fuel type can be found anywhere.

Personally, I use Gaz, which makes a very simple, high-powered stove. I paid $33 for it. There are limitations (extreme cold and high winds), but I don't exceed those limitations. It's perfect for me. For a better selection of stoves that perform under extreme conditions and have refillable gas canisters, look through a Primus or MSR catalog at your nearest backpacking store or online.

CHAPTER 11

PREP AT HOME

Getting prepared at home is the single most important thing you can do to improve your meals. Preparing can be something you do six minutes before you leave or something you can do days, weeks, or even months in advance. If you enjoy backpacking as much as I do, then going on a trip is always in the back of your mind. Instead of letting that idea sit complacently in your head, do something about it. If you know you can't go backpacking for a while, start getting ready anyway. There's always work to be done, and the more you do, the easier it will be to get your butt off the couch and outside on the trail where it belongs.

Packing truly is one of the great deterrents to getting out, and getting your food ready is the most tedious part. On the morning of your trip you think of all the meals you'd really like to eat and how much trouble it's going to be to get them ready. You start to wonder, "Why bother?" Suddenly you find yourself wanting to see movies that you've never heard of or go out to that restaurant you hate just to give it one last chance. Even worse, out of nowhere you notice what a mess your place is, start cleaning, and can't find a way to stop until it's too late.

If you can't relate to this, consider yourself extremely lucky. Nothing in the world is more depressing than to anxiously await your backpacking trip for weeks until it comes time to pack up your stuff. You end up sitting around all night even though you promised yourself it would never happen. Another missed opportunity at adding an incredible memory to your life. Help yourself by getting everything organized and in place—ready to go in an instant. You might still end up on the couch from time to time, but I guarantee it won't happen as much as it used to.

The other huge reason to get food ready in the off-season, or when the weather is horrible, is because you eat a lot better. Early last summer I dedicated a couple of hours to chopping mushrooms, asparagus, zucchini, and onions to throw in the dehydrator. Of course it seems like a monumental task at first, but somehow it only takes a few short hours at the most to get a food supply ready for a whole summer. Yes, that's right, a whole summer. Every time I wanted to spend a night out, I had a bin full of food begging to go into my pack. I had a nice bag of Cream of Wheat with sugar, powdered milk, and cinnamon mixed in. Next to it I had a small bag to put it in for one, two, or however many nights I wanted to spend out. I had four Ziplocs full of dried veggies that weighed only a couple of ounces apiece, just waiting to get mixed into a stir fry bag. Also in the box were some pasta, instant rice, trail mix, and lots more. Everything right down to soy sauce, salt and pepper, and clean forks and spoons lived in that box. I didn't have to do much other than pick up a couple of candy bars at the store or rummage through my fridge for a couple of bagels and some cream cheese.

The hardest part was staying out of the pancake mix while I was at home. My food was actually good—a thousand times better than it's ever been before. I had pasta that didn't have to be done much differently outside than at home when I'm trying to impress the ladies. I had stir fry with mushrooms, asparagus, onions, soy sauce, ginger, and cashews—and I didn't even stop at the store before the trip. Sure, macaroni and cheese can be good sometimes, but the food I had was good all the time, and a hell of a lot more nutritious than any volatile packet full of glowing orange cheese dust. Plus you don't have to worry about aliens spotting your glowing cheese dust from space and using a beam to suck you up for extensive scientific testing, wondering why in the name of all that's holy you would deliberately put such a toxic substance into your body.

HERBS, SPICES, & COOKING SUPPLIES

Herbs and spices, as you know, don't weigh very much, but that still doesn't mean you should bring an army of them to attack your food. Packing herbs, spices, and other seasonings is like anything else: only bring what you will use. That means you should have some idea of what you're going to eat. If you know you want pasta for dinner and some oatmeal for breakfast, don't bring the whole container of cinnamon from your cabinet and a small glass spice jar full of dried basil to go on your pasta. Only bring what you need. I'd suggest throwing some brown sugar and cinnamon in with your bag of oats. You've got everything you need for that meal except water. What if you want raisins and milk and butter in it too? No problem—throw in some raisins, some powdered milk, and bring along a small container of butter (I'd recommend grabbing or buying a few extra butter packets every time you see one at a restaurant or something). The same goes for other condiments that you like: mayo, ketchup, mustard, honey, and cream cheese are a real score—shhh, don't tell anyone I told you that.

If you want packing to be easy all summer and your food to taste better, get some of the things you commonly use to cook with ready ahead of time. Keep your potential dry goods all in one box, ready to be thrown together. It's like a little food-packing set. The following is a list of ingredients that I keep in my food box, but your choice of nonperishable items is up to you.

- salt and pepper
- cooking oil
- flavored oil(s) (olive, sesame, truffle—depending on what you plan to use)
- seasoning mixes
- Asian sauces (soy sauce, ponzu, hoisin, sweet chili sauce, etc.)
- hot sauce or cayenne pepper
- sweets (sugar, maple syrup, honey)
- vinegar
- powdered soy milk (or powdered milk)
- whole wheat flour
- homemade dehydrated produce (corn, zucchini, asparagus, peas, broccoli, etc.)
- store-bought dehydrated produce (sun-dried tomatoes, raisins, craisins, etc.)
- baking powder
- condiment packets
- angel-hair pasta
- couscous
- instant rice
- instant black and refried beans
- instant hummus
- instant mashed potatoes
- ramen noodles
- Cream of Wheat
- cornmeal
- oats
- Ziploc bags
- spoons, forks, and pocketknife

CHAPTER 12

REDUCING TRASH

When you transfer cereal to a plastic bag and leave the big paperboard box at home, you're not just reducing what you're carrying in, but also what you're carrying out. Packaging takes up space, and the weight can add up. When you decide to bring a jar of strawberry jelly, you have to remember that once you've eaten it, you still have to carry out that big jar. An important aspect of packing your meals for a trip is coming up with a strategy that allows your pack to become smaller and lighter as your trip progresses. Bringing your food in separate plastic bags pays off in several ways. Your food is organized and easy to prepare once you get to your campsite; you can bring only the amount you need; your trash is light, compact, and clean; you can reuse most of the bags trip after trip; and odors are reduced.

Minimizing the amount of packaging is important primarily because you don't have to carry excess stuff in your pack. First of all, try to buy foods that don't have a lot of packaging in the first place. Even if the packaging materials are recyclable, time, money, and energy are wasted in the recycling process. It will also make your packing easier. The simple steps to reducing packaging couldn't be easier. Leave boxes, jars, cartons, and cans at home if at all possible, or avoid packaging entirely by buying in bulk. Although there are exceptions, a good rule of thumb is if you can read it, you should leave it. That means that if the packaging has the nutrition facts, ingredients, and brand name on it, it can probably be reduced into a smaller, lighter, resealable container. Stay-fresh, built-in seals in the packaging are exceptions, and it is important to pick these out at the store so you don't have to use any more plastic bags. The downside to leaving packaging at home is that you lose any directions for preparation that might come in handy later. Fix this problem by labeling things yourself, with cooking directions if necessary.

Another important reason not to bring the package your food is sold in is because it probably wasn't sold in the amount you'll need for a trip. On a two-day trip, unless you're a fanatic, you won't need an entire jar of peanut butter, not even one of the small ones. If you must bring heavy, messy peanut butter, transfer the amount you'll need to a smaller plastic container or plastic bag. If you are going on a week-long trip and the amount of peanut butter in the plastic container at the store looks like the right amount, go ahead. The idea is to end the trip with only a few handfuls of Granola still left in your pack. Of course, having a little too much is better than not quite having enough, but with a little practice, you should be able to plan it out perfectly.

Keeping everything in sealable containers is also very important for reducing odors and keeping things clean. Making a huge mess at home isn't much of a problem with a drawer full of towels and nice warm water coming out of the faucet, but in the backcountry it's a different story. The worst things you can possibly bring are canned meats. Everything is fine and dandy, except for the weight of the load in your pack, until you open the can and eat the tuna or, heaven forbid, the Spam. Once you open that can you have a nice potent meat smell trapped in your pack, not only bothering you but attracting bears. The alternative is to put these meats in a plastic bag beforehand, which is even worse because the meat no longer has its tin shell to preserve it. Unless canned meat is simply too enticing, I'd recommend leaving it at home. They are starting to pack tuna in sealed bags, but if you're going on a long trip, the inside of that bag is going to reek of rotten fish in just a few short days—something to keep in mind.

On long trips, any perishable food by-products such as pits, stems, peels, or what have you will also get really stinky if you don't keep them sealed up in a Ziploc. As many of us have learned the hard way, strong smells attract hungry animals. Ziploc bags function in food organization and transport, and they make great garbage bags for a smart backpacker—sealing in odors much better than thin plastic sacks. No matter how long you're out, a large Ziploc should be enough for all of your trash if you plan right. Reducing your packaging seems easy, but it really takes some thought to get it perfect. Here are some general tips for leaving as much at home as possible:

Use the same foods in several meals while you're out

If you bring a bag of raisins, use them in oatmeal, Cream of Wheat, and as a snack. You can even mix them in with your bag of oats, Cream of Wheat, and trail mix at home to avoid having to bring a separate bag. You can mix dried cherries into your rice, raisins in your trail mix, and dried blueberries in your pancake mix, adding variety to your meals without having to bring three separate bags for each kind of dried fruit, berry, vegetable, herb, or mushroom.

Consolidate like items

What if you get ready at the last minute and all you have to eat is three pre-packaged backpacker meals? If they're all the same, try throwing all of them into the same bag, and leave the metal-lined packages at home. The same applies to other things that are alike. Why carry out three packages when you could carry out one?

Mix things together

If you're having pasta for dinner on a short trip, don't bring a bag with basil, one with sun-dried tomatoes, one with parmesan, and one with garlic powder. Mix them all together, and throw in a little salt and pepper. Cook your pasta, add the mix, and let it sit for a bit before digging in. You could have brought seven bags if you include the salt and pepper. Now you've cut it down to just two.

Always, always, ALWAYS be thinking into the future

This can be strenuous for the human mind, especially if you're a politician, but it can be done, and it pays off. Decide what you're going to eat while you're packing or even before. Don't decide once you're out there. If you are dying for peanut butter and jelly, then bring some in two Nalgene plastic containers. It doesn't make sense to bring these two huge containers for a couple of peanut butter and jelly sandwiches though, right? No it doesn't, unless you plan to use them for other things once the peanut butter and jelly are gone. Wash them out after your PBJs and use them for soup one night, store leftover pasta for pasta salad the next day, and use them to keep burritos in after you scrape "Mexican Night" leftovers into a couple of tortillas. Just think, "If I'm going to bring this thing, how else can I use it?" Ask that question and you'll be better off than ever before. For example, if you want to bring a frying pan for pancakes, bring other foods that can be cooked in the frying pan, like quesadillas, so that you can leave your pot behind. Try to think about things in this way, and you'll stay one step ahead.

CHAPTER 13

FUEL ALTERNATIVES

CRO-MAGNON COOKING

This type of cooking is considered old-fashioned. So old-fashioned that I threw it in the caveman category. What am I talking about? The campfire, you little Girl Scout you. I don't do a lot of campfire cooking, but what I have done has been the tastiest and the easiest. Plus, you can do some things over the open fire that you just can't do with a simple gas stove and pot. I'm not recommending that you throw away your stove and all your pots and pans; I'm just saying that if you think you might be "pyro-ing" in the forest on your trip, then take some stuff to utilize that heat. That's right, use it, friend, don't just stare at it and drool.

Let me repeat this point one more time. Don't rely 100% on the campfire for your cooking needs. In this day and age, it's nearly impossible. There are several places where campfires are not allowed or are restricted in some way. During dry months, there may be a fire ban in the area you're in. Some campsites just won't have any wood around to use except for live stuff, and if I catch you chopping down live trees to roast your weenies and marshmallows, I will inflict harm upon you, with the help of Jean Claude of course. All I'm saying is that if you know you're going to build the bonfire, then don't let it go to waste. Bring the weenies, the marshmallows, and the chocolate if you have no respect for your body. If you do have some respect for your internal organs, bring some garlic, some bell peppers, some onions, or anything else roastable.

Other than what you intend to roast, all you might need is some seasonings, oil, and aluminum foil. I really like the aluminum foil trick. Whatever you want to roast and later consume, wrap tightly inside the foil and throw it in the fire right next to some medium-hot coals. Garlic is a favorite. I cover whole heads with a light layer of oil, wrap them in foil, and then toss it on in.

Rotate it every few minutes or so to keep from having one burnt side and one raw side, and "boo-yah," you've got roasted garlic—and you still get to stare at the fire the whole time, poking your shiny aluminum object with a stick. Of course, you may blow it the first time or two. The coals may have been too hot or too cold, you may have left the garlic in for too long or not long enough, but you'll get the hang of it, and it's fun and tasty—tantamount to any s'more I've ever concocted.

Other things you can roast in the same way are whole or cut potatoes or other starchy vegetables (turnips, parsnips, carrots, celery root, etc.), bell peppers, onions, shallots, tomatoes, zucchini, and more. You might also experiment with fruit. Throw sugar and cinnamon on some sliced peaches, apples, and walnuts, let it roast for a while, and oh yeah, baby! You've got yourself a little fancy dessert now, don't ya' Mr. Fancy Pants. Shoot, for a one-nighter you could marinate some steaks and throw dem steaks on dat dair fire.

Moving right along… Other things I like to cook in aluminum foil are fresh-caught trout and hot sandwiches. For the trout, I usually season them up with salt, pepper, and a little cayenne, line the outsides with sliced lemons and garlic, squirt them with oil, wrap them up in foil, briefly cook each side directly over the flame, and then move them to a cooler spot to finish cooking. Got all that? Or you can just put them on a stick and roast them like you would a marshmallow or weenie, making sure they get fully cooked on the inside. This gives them a great smoky flavor.

Hot sandwiches are wickedly good too. First, toast a bagel over the open flame, and then, between the two halves, put whatever you like—meat, tuna, cheese, sliced tomatoes, avocado, precooked bacon, tofu, condiments, you name it. Then, wrap it in aluminum foil and set it over medium-hot coals for a long time, until everything in the middle is melted and steaming. Just don't burn the bagel by putting it somewhere that's too hot. Keep checking her if you have to, but try to avoid it. Checking the sammy every 19 seconds is a sure way to get ashes all over it. Nobody likes an ash sandwich. "Oooo gross, this sandwich tastes like somebody's ash!"

Finally, in the Cro-Magnon section, every caveman and cavewoman's favorite technique: the put-on-a-stick-and-rotate roast. Bring out the mallows, whip out your wieners … or wait, on second thought, please don't do that. Just like the trout, if you can find a way to get it stuck on a stick, you should be able to roast it, no problem. Another advantage of stick roasting is that you don't have to pack out a big wad of food-covered aluminum foil that rots and festers in some lonely Ziploc. Plus, the primitive caveman-ish charm of stick roasting is priceless. Just don't start beating your woman with a wooden club, dragging her around by her hair, or speaking in broken sentence fragments. "Squirrel liver good. Fire hot. Woman pretty. Dave stinky, need shower."

I LIKE IT RAW

Another option, which I have discussed in little snippets here and there, is the possibility of not cooking your food. Now, when I say this you're probably envisioning a bloody, slimy chicken leg or something. No, no, I'm just talking about bringing foods that you don't need to cook. I do this very often in winter or on short trips. If I'm only going to have a couple meals where I'll be able to cook something, it seems kind of stupid to carry along a stove, eating utensils, pot, and fuel. It's easier and lighter to leave that crap at home and stick to the precooked or raw edibles. For a cook-free trip, you might bring items such as:

- granola
- cereal
- powdered milk
- trail mix
- dried fruit/fruit rolls/fresh fruit or berries
- nuts
- jerky
- smoked salmon, lox, canned tuna, crab, etc.
- olives
- capers
- pickles
- crackers
- cheeses
- chips
- cookies, candy bars, and other yummy tooth-rotters
- bagels
- bread
- luncheon meats
- peanut butter and jelly
- tortillas and salsa
- fresh and dried vegetables to add to sandwiches, crackers, bagels, etc.
- olive oil, butter, or cream cheese to add to bagels and sandwiches
- a few items for cooking over a campfire

As you can see, your options are not really all that limited. Even the ingredients here can be improvised and messed around with to make incredible dishes. For short trips, it is really not a bad idea to bring preprepared raw foods. A vegetable salad might be great. At home, quarter and seed some roma tomatoes and steam a little asparagus. Mix them in a bowl with extra-virgin olive oil, salt and pepper, fresh basil, croutons, pine nuts, and crumbled feta cheese. Bring your lovely fresh creation in a sturdy plastic container and enjoy it for dinner with some French bread.

For breakfast, have cereal with dried berries and yogurt. Have Granola with milk (made from powdered milk and filtered water). Try just a plain old bagel with cream cheese or jelly, or bring some capers, onion, and salmon lox. Does that really sound worse than oatmeal?

For desserts, eat your usual cookies, chocolates, and candy, or try a light raw food adventure—diced nectarines, strawberries, and apples with pecans, brown sugar, cinnamon, and vanilla.

For snacks, lunches, and even dinners, bring a snazzy spreadable cheese like Allouette or Montrachet. Spread the cheese on a cracker and top with a sliced Kalamata olive, a little rehydrated sun-dried tomato, and a slice of smoked salmon. Try the same on a baguette—maybe even heat it up over a campfire.

I'm not trying to scare anyone with fancy French words and obscure ingredients, I'm just trying to show you that you can still get gourmet on that ass without a stove. Going without cookware is fun, easy, and it doesn't mean that you'll be tearing miserably at jerky all day, dreaming of the moist delicious cuisine that you once knew. Good food awaits you. Try it sometime.

CHAPTER 14

PERFECT RECIPES

Yes, perfect recipes. I know it sounds like I'm a little full of myself, but these recipes really are pretty damn good for a backpacker. They use very little fuel, and can be done in one pot—the trail mix doesn't need to be cooked at all. None of them are exquisite or exotic in any way, so they are simple, good enough, and make sense for someone with a limited kitchen. They are also packed with the things you need: vitamins, minerals, calories, carbohydrates, fat, and protein. Not to sound like your mom, but you need these things in massive quantities when your days are full of rigorous exercise. Anyway, try them, tweak them to your liking, and use some of the ideas here to create ideas of your own—pasta sauces, soups, vegetable curries, other breakfast cereals, homemade power bars, and so on, and so on…

COUSCOUS CHILI: SERVES 2

Ingredients
¾ cup couscous
¼ cup instant rice
Bean and spice mix:
2 T chili powder
2 t ground coriander
2 t ground cumin
¼ cup instant black or instant refried beans
¼ cup crushed corn tortilla chips
Dehydrated mix:
¼ cup tomato paste
2 ears of corn—cut into niblets
2 oz. diced green chiles

Raw ingredients:
- juice of 1 lime
- 2 diced shallots
- 2 minced cloves of garlic
- 2 T extra-virgin olive oil

Preparation

At home, dehydrate tomato paste, corn, and green chiles by mixing together, thinning out with water until it's easily spreadable, and putting on a dehydrator. Also make a bean and spice mix using instant beans—good ones are made by Fantastic Foods Inc., and can be found at almost any large supermarket.

At camp, sauté shallots and garlic in olive oil, adding both the dehydrated mix and the bean-spice mix when shallots and garlic just start to turn brown. Mix well and add 3 cups water. Once it has come to a boil, add lime juice, salt and pepper, and the couscous and instant rice. Cover and let set for up to 10 minutes, stirring every 2 or 3 minutes until chili is thick. Thin with filtered water if necessary.

TRAIL MIX: YIELDS 6 CUPS

Ingredients
- 1 cup whole almonds
- 1 cup peanuts
- 2 cups dried fruit (cherries, raisins, apricots, apples, dates, figs, cranberries, etc.)
- 1 cup flaked coconut or sweetened coconut
- 1 cup Granola

Preparation
Mix all ingredients well in a large bowl. Put in a large Ziploc bag and snack it up. Keep in freezer for long-term storage.

APPLE-CRANBERRY OATMEAL: SERVES 2

Ingredients
- ¼ cup chopped dried apple
- ¼ cup dried cranberries
- 1¼ cup whole rolled oats (*not* instant oats)
- 3 T brown sugar
- ¼ t salt
- 1 t cinnamon
- 2 T powdered milk or soy milk

Preparation

Mix all ingredients at home and place in a Ziploc bag. At camp, boil 2½ cups water, add the oatmeal mix, turn off heat, and cover with a lid. Stir every 2 minutes for 6 minutes. Add ½ cup Granola or trail mix before serving.

PARMESAN POLENTA: SERVES 2
Ingredients

2½ cups water
½ cup powdered milk or soy milk
½ cup white cornmeal (yellow works also but doesn't taste as good)
½ cup grated parmesan cheese
2 T butter

Preparation

Bring water to a boil and add powdered milk or soy milk. Stir in cornmeal and turn heat to low. Stir frequently and keep cooking until it gets thick (5–10 minutes). Turn off heat, stir in butter, add salt and pepper to taste, and then add cheese. Serve as a breakfast porridge or to accompany whatever you're having for dinner. Can also be cooled and fried in about a tablespoon of oil.

INDIAN CURRY: SERVES 2
Ingredients

Dehydrated mix:
½ cup dehydrated peas (not split peas—those take forever to cook)
¼ cup dehydrated broccoli
¼ cup instant mashed potatoes
¼ cup golden raisins
¼ cup whole almonds
1 T curry powder
Separate Ingredients:
2 T Massaman or other curry paste (Mae-Ploy is the best brand available)
1 T chopped ginger
1 t chopped garlic
1 T chopped shallot
2 T olive oil

Preparation

First make some plain couscous or instant rice and set aside in a separate plastic container—covered to help keep it warm. For the curry, rinse and dry your pot and start by sautéing ginger, garlic, shallot, and curry paste in olive oil. Add dehydrated mix and 3 cups water. Bring to a boil and simmer for 1 minute. Cover and let sit for at least 5 minutes to let the vegetables rehydrate. Serve curry over your rice or couscous.

SIMPLE PASTA WITH TOMATO SAUCE: SERVES 2

Ingredients
Dehydrated sauce:
- 6 ounces tomato paste
- ½ small yellow onion; roughly chopped
- 5 cloves garlic
- 10 large basil leaves
- water

Separate Ingredients:
- ½ pound angel-hair pasta
- 2 T extra-virgin olive oil
- 1 T butter
- ¼ cup grated parmesan

Preparation

At home, prepare the pasta sauce by mixing the chopped onion, tomato paste, and garlic together in a pot. Add water until it is slightly thinner than the desired consistency. Cook on low heat for 30–45 minutes, add whole basil leaves and salt and pepper to taste. Puree the mixture roughly in a blender, then pour the sauce onto the plastic sheets that come with most dehydrators. Let dry until the sauce is hard and peels from the plastic. At camp, heat olive oil, add the dried sauce, cover with water, bring to a boil, and let sit to rehydrate while you cook your pasta. Finally, check the consistency of your sauce, stir in butter, and mix with your cooked pasta. Top with grated cheese.

PART V

DANGER, DANGER, DANGER!

Let's see,
site 12,
where's site 12?

I took out a five-year-old photo of the campsite. In the background I could see the lake far below. Immediately it became obvious where the site was—up on the steep hill on the east side of the lake. I hurried up the hill. The light rain was now turning to fat moist flakes of snow. The sooner I made it back to camp the better—before the slick coat of water on the rocks froze over and became even more treacherous. Hustling up the trail I veered off and found the last campsite on the inventory list. Site 12.

The photo showed a small tree stump, roots still attached, bleached by the sun, laying flat on the ground near a small pile of black campfire coals. I looked up and there it was. The coals were covered with a thin layer of green moss; the rest of the site covered with grass, now turned brown with winter approaching. The tree stump had hardly changed a bit, although it was now facing a slightly different direction where someone, or something, had moved it. Even though number 12 lay right beside the trail where any passerby in search of a place to camp could see it, it looked completely abandoned. I took out a pencil and wrote "Site 12 Revegetated" in large ugly handwriting in the middle of a campsite inventory form, which I did with hundreds of these forms as one of my wilderness ranger duties, among other things. I folded up the inventory notebook, put it in my backpack, and set out to return to camp—quickly.

The light snow turned heavy. Clouds fell into the valley as they reached the ridges on either side, closing down on me, transforming into ever closer fog. The grass looked more brown than before. The brilliant yellow aspen leaves from my hike up looked more dead. Their leaves looked sickly and wilted. They no longer quaked in the breeze, but hung limply as the thick cement fell from the sky. I pulled my green hood over my head and stared at the wet mud right in front of my feet, trying to place each footstep in a secure spot. Things were getting slippery, and the trail itself was officially unmaintained—good because I didn't have to do any work, but at the same time it was a disaster. Huge roots stuck up out of steep, eroded, rocky sections. Fallen trees covered the trail. Water was using the trail as a canal, making things muddy and slick, and it was narrow and bowl-shaped, making it impossible to walk normally.

I kept focusing on the mud in front of my feet and nothing else. As I descended, the storm eased up. By the time I made it back to the lake things had calmed down. All was quiet, and I removed my hood to listen to the silence.

Low clouds were no longer falling down the hillsides. They just hung there motionless, below the ridge, like dangling, upside-down double-scoop vanilla cones. Wetness covered everything, and the valley behind me was now dusted with white. Winter had shown its face, but retreated to let life take one last breath.

The chill of cold air invaded my wet jacket and the wetness underneath. It was time to get back to the tent. The only thing standing between me and my tent was a field of jagged wet boulders. I had crossed it on the way up without any difficulty, but everything was slick, wet, maybe even iced over. I tiptoed out onto the rocks. The surface of the boulders was rough, and the traction felt secure. I tried to keep my boots as flat as I could on the rocks for the best hold. Near the end of the boulder field was a particularly jagged section. There were no flat rocks to step on. I approached the first of the boulders, crouching low and using my hands for extra support. My feet followed the lead of my upper body, and I found myself stretched out like a champion "Twister" player, with each limb on a different rock. No problem.

Reaching the end I noticed a particularly slippery one. I put my left foot on a more secure rock and then leaned towards it, using my hands for extra support as I reached out timidly toward the slick one with my right foot. With all worries on the fate of my right foot, and too much invested in the left, I paid for my mistake. In an instant the left foot gave out, and my body was turned completely horizontal to the ground—falling. A pointed rock below was the first thing to slow my momentum. It thrust into my ribcage between my stomach and heart at about the same time that my brain realized I was falling. The bones bent under the pressure, and withstood the blow, but the pain made me think otherwise. I let out a horrible moan like that of a sexually frustrated elk during mating season. Was I alright? Could I breathe? I painfully tried to inflate my empty lungs. My breaths were short and panicked. My knee was aching with pain, and I was having trouble moving it. I sank down in the rocks and curled up, one hand on my knee, the other on my ribs. The lake was silent and the gray skies were darkening. The only sound I could hear was a chilling breeze blowing through the dying aspen leaves behind me.

Fifteen seconds later the worst of the pain was on its way out. I could feel the pain releasing, like I had hoped it would, and my fear faded away. My breathing was difficult, but all was functioning well enough to survive. Luckily, my tent was only 100 yards away, it was already set up, and all I had to do was crawl in pitifully and sleep off the pain.

In all, my body fell about three feet. It sounds pathetic, but imagine someone holding your body sideways over an empty, shallow swimming pool. The pool is full of cone-shaped rocks. Suddenly, you are released. Before you have time to react the sharp rocks are crashing into your soft flesh and fragile bones.

All I was doing was walking. Walking, that's all backpacking really is, and it is actually dangerous, because one very awkward fall, miles from help, in harsh conditions, can leave you helplessly waiting for rescue—unable to help yourself in any way.

If someone had videotaped my whole ordeal by the lake that day, I would probably watch it with friends over and over again, laughing until my side hurt almost as bad as it did that day. But the fall changed my view of the backcountry. For the first time in my life I wondered, even though it was only for 15 seconds, whether or not I would still be around the next day. I tried to be cautious, I was doing everything I felt I could do at the moment, and if that rock was a little sharper, it could have cracked ribs and sent them into my vital organs—with no help anywhere, and a cold wet night approaching. It was terrifying—like having a real-life Jason standing above me with chainsaw and hockey mask, while I lay helpless on the ground, powerless to do anything to defend myself—unable to escape death, too late to change nature's course.

Okay, let's lighten up a bit. I didn't write an entire book dedicated to motivating you to go backpacking, just to screw it up here. Look on the bright side. All those things you're worried about, such as animal attacks, snakebites, lightning strikes, and hypothermia are all easy to prevent. If you don't do anything stupid, you'll be fine. Most things are under your control. If you do it the right way, you've got little to worry about. Freak accidents happen, of course, but if you're worried that backpacking is too dangerous, then get a grip on reality. The exercise alone will improve your health. Millions of people die each year, and one of the contributing causes to their death is failure to exercise.

If you are really paranoid about death, you should never drive your car, eat another burger, or smoke another cigarette ever again. You'd be much safer spending the rest of your life backpacking around, breathing fresh air, and exercising every day. And when it comes to my personal pet peeve—fear of animal attack—I wouldn't worry much. The most dangerous one out there is the infamous *homo sapiens*.

The most dangerous thing you will face, hands down, however lame it may sound, will be your own ability to walk. This is of course if you've remembered all essential equipment items, have stored your food properly, are familiar with maps and know how to use a compass, know how to take cover during lightning storms, and let yourself properly acclimatize to elevation gain. These are the things you can control and will be the focus of the following chapters. I can't help you much with the walking. If you need instruction, this book won't even begin to be able to address your problems, so I've decided to let you figure this one out on your own instead of pretending like there's some secret foolproof technique. I usually stick with right, and then left. I hear left, and then right also works well. Most importantly, drive safely on your way to the trailhead.

CHAPTER 15

NATURE'S HAZARDS

CHILL OUT

Hypothermia, better known as freezing your ass off, is probably the greatest danger to an unprepared backpacker. People die from hypothermia more frequently than they should, and more frequently in the warmer months than in the colder months. Why? The first reason is that more people are out trooping around when it's warm than when it's cold. The second reason is that people usually prepare themselves better for cold temperatures and assume they'll be fine in shorts and a T-shirt in the summer no matter what happens. The third reason is that water, when it's really cold outside, falls from the sky in the form of snow, which won't get you nearly as wet as rain. Wet clothes equal a cold body, and you have a much greater chance of getting wet in the summer than the winter—in most places.

So what is hypothermia, besides being really cold? Well, what happens is your core temperature begins to drop. When this happens you lose control of your body, and then, as your temperature continues to drop, you gradually lose control of your mind. A little hypothermia, if you are warmed up right away and taken care of, isn't terribly serious if you're a healthy person. The scariest side of hypothermia is that you begin to lose your ability to think clearly and rationally. You might forget that you're cold and that you need help. I've heard that some people have even felt hot once hypothermia has fully set in, and actually remove clothing to cool off. The point is that once you get too cold, you become powerless to help yourself. Yes, it's unfortunate, I know.

To protect yourself from hypothermia, you must stay warm and dry. It's quite simple and easy. It's also quite simple and easy to misjudge the weather or forget your warm clothes or assume you will be fine even though you've been informed of all the dangers. Things can go wrong, too. Your raincoat may not work, you may fall down in a river, your backpack may roll down a hill into a lake—soaking your down sleeping bag and all your warm clothes—and so on. As a backpacker, you do have one advantage, though—you bring everything you need. A day-hiker or someone close to safety may assume that there is no danger of hypothermia. You will have a giant backpack and you will be prepared for a number of weather conditions.

So, to stay warm and dry, bring a raincoat, a jacket or fleece, a sleeping bag, and a tent or some other rainproof covering. If you're traveling in winter, bring the same items as well as extra warm clothes, including warm, waterproof pants, boots, and gloves, which are more or less optional in summer. Unfortunately, bringing all these things is not enough. You have to keep them dry too. Keeping them inside your backpack will help. Backpacks will probably never be 100% rainproof, but they do help. For extra protection you can pack essential items in waterproof stuff sacks sold at most backpacking stores, or just use plain old plastic trash bags and Ziplocs. You can also use a pack cover, which costs about 30 bucks and keeps not only your gear dry, but your backpack also. If you're really concerned, use a pack cover and waterproof stuff sacks. You should be safe unless you fall in a river and lay there for a few minutes with backpack submerged.

If you do get hypothermia, or someone you are traveling with slips into it, it's important to get them "warming up" immediately. Notice that I didn't say "warmed up." Go slowly. Your body really wants to ease into things. Throwing someone in hypothermia into a hot bathtub is going to make their problems worse. A gradual warm-up is best. The most important thing is that they are not getting progressively colder. If body temperature drops too low it can damage some cherished parts of your physiology. Removing wet clothing and getting yourself or your friend into a dry sleeping bag should fix the problem. If it doesn't seem to be working, snuggle with a warmer companion or put some warm water in water bottles, and use them as sleeping bag warmers. Once again, make sure that nothing is too hot. No "hot" drinks, no "hot" water, etc. Warm up as slowly as possible to ease the adjustment that your body has to make.

HEAT EXHAUSTION/HEATSTROKE

Getting too cold is a big concern in some locales, but in others, getting too hot is the greater danger. Heat exhaustion is dangerous. Like hypothermia, once your body temperature has changed drastically, it is hard to bring it back to normal. If you are out on a hot day, the sun is beating down, there is no shade, there is no water, and perhaps you are already dehydrated, further preventing you from sweating and cooling off—you are in real trouble. Heat exhaustion is the first form of overheating, where your body stops sweating and you get dizzy and overly fatigued. The important thing to do at this point is find shade and water and stop pushing yourself up those steep hills in the sun. Perhaps you are in the desert and it's not possible to find such a place, but do what you can to cool off. Pour water on yourself, drink water to rehydrate your body, and fan yourself with a T-shirt, your hand, or whatever you can find.

Heat exhaustion is not necessarily hazardous to your health. It will weaken you, draining your body of energy and further preventing your natural cooling system from working. The real danger is heatstroke, which can happen if you don't heed the warning signs sent out by heat exhaustion. Heatstroke is a complete shutdown of the body, where your body temperature climbs far too high, endangering your internal organs, and eventually, if you don't start cooling down right away, killing you. Like hypothermia, once you have gotten past a certain point you are unable to help yourself. It is essential to react to early warning signs and be prepared to cool yourself off when traveling in a hot environment. Also, like hypothermia, you must not shock your body by trying to cool off too quickly. Jumping in an icy stream while you are suffering from heat exhaustion or heatstroke can't be good for ya. Cool off slowly and let your body adjust and come down on its own.

UP HIGH

Altitude is a serious concern, and you don't have to be climbing Everest to get spanked by it. Altitude sickness can affect people at elevations as low as 8,000 feet, and sometimes even lower than that. Mild altitude sickness produces symptoms such as headache, nausea, loss of appetite, dizziness, and other indicators that your body turns on to say, "Hey, what the hell are you doing to me? Stop now or I will make you pay so help me God!" And yes, your body will make you pay if you don't head downhill in a hurry. The worst-case scenario is bleeding in the brain and lungs, which at best will leave you with a lot of pain, a huge medical bill, and irreversible damage to some of your most prized organs.

To stop this horrendous process from taking place in your body, you must do several things. First of all, don't climb to a high elevation right away. If you've just come from sea level, a rapid ascent to the top of a 14,000-foot peak will wipe you out, even if you've climbed Everest before. Second, if you do attempt to pull off a feat like this, at least drop some elevation before camping for the night. Spending an entire night 14,000 feet higher than where you spent your last night is very dangerous. Once you're above 10,000 feet you shouldn't increase your camping elevation by more than 1,000 feet per night if you're not at all acclimatized—meaning that you've been at high elevations for quite some time and your body is used to decreased oxygen levels. Third, do everything you can to make sure that your body can give full attention to acclimatizing: drink plenty of water, keep pumping in the calories, don't overexert yourself physically, don't let yourself get too hot or cold, etc.

Another thing that gets people in trouble is thinking that if they have lived at high altitudes, or done a lot of backpacking in the past, they are somehow immune to high elevations. If you were raised in Denver and have spent the last 10 years living in Florida, your body will not take a rapid ascent to 13,000 feet very kindly. In fact, as soon as you descend elevation, you are once again susceptible to getting altitude sickness. It's true that your body will adjust slightly if it's used to going up and down in elevation all the time, but not as much as some people think. The key to prevention of altitude sickness is taking it seriously. If you have a slight headache, don't panic, but don't push yourself when it comes to elevation. If you are really feeling it—and trust me, you'll be 100% sure if you're really feeling it—you'll feel like you're about to keel over, and your heart will race with every footstep, then take it easy. Go down, camp another night at a lower elevation, and try climbing uphill again the next day. By then, you'll be strengthened and ready. And, if you're feeling the altitude where you are, don't just decide that that's enough and set up camp. Go downhill 1,000 feet or two. You'll feel better, be safer, and sleep much better.

LET LIGHTNING STRIKE ME DOWN

Lightning doesn't sound that scary, because you know your chances of getting struck just aren't that good. There are, however, ways that you can greatly increase your chances, especially when tromping around through high mountains and open meadows. So make sure not to do anything stupid. Lightning, although there are exceptions to everything, tends to strike the highest objects around. The key to avoiding lightning couldn't be more simple—don't let yourself be the tallest thing around. Don't frolic across open meadows while bolts are striking close by. Don't cross high passes above tree line during a nasty thunderstorm, don't cruise out onto a lake in a canoe, and so on.

When lightning is getting really nasty—and you'll know if it's nasty by the frantic pounding of your heart as you wonder where the next incredibly loud bolt will strike, get down low. Most lightning safety information I've seen recommends that you squat down with only the balls of your feet touching the ground. This is to protect you not only from getting struck right on top of the noggin, but also to protect you from electricity passing through the ground from nearby strikes. Another tip is to keep all metal away from you. Most backpacks have metal "stays" in them to give the frame support. These are bad to have on you in a lightning storm. Separate yourself from your backpack no matter how nice it would be to sit down on it instead of squatting. You've probably got tent poles, metal cookware, stakes, and all kinds of lightning attractants in there too, so ditch that thing. And be patient. Your legs will hurt, and you'll want to get up and start walking again. Let the lightning dictate when you hustle out of there, not your knees.

From personal experience sitting through lightning storms, I believe that hypothermia is a much more legitimate danger. Cold rain pours down on you while you sit there, motionless, for sometimes a half hour or more. The closest I've ever come to slipping into hypothermia—and I might have actually been experiencing some of the early symptoms, was waiting out a lightning storm. My rain gear was crappy and I knew that ahead of time. By myself, I would have said screw it and crossed the small field to get back to camp, but I was with four other people and they wanted to wait. So I waited with them. By the time we did cross the small meadow, I could barely walk. My muscle control was fading, and I didn't feel completely warm until the next morning—even after roasting in front of a campfire half the night and sipping hot chocolate.

Oh yeah, and don't set up your tent on the top of a peak or in an open meadow no matter how clear the sky is when you get there. Thunder cracking in the night while your tent is pitched in a field is dangerous and also prevents sleep from occurring.

RIVER CROSSINGS

Rivers can be pretty scary. They can look so gentle and benign, but turn out to be furiously powerful. Small creeks and streams are usually not much of a problem. If the water is at knee level or below, it's hard to really get yourself in trouble. The only way to drown yourself there is to fall and hit your head—which is much easier on slick rocks with moving water crashing into your legs than it is under normal circumstances. Face it, rivers are dangerous, even the small ones.

For bigger, major river crossings, you must be equipped. First of all, I would recommend avoiding any kind of major river crossing. Even if you do make it across your gear might get wet, you may not be able to get back successfully, and so on. If you can avoid crossing it, then do so.

If you absolutely must make it to the other side for whatever reason, make sure you are not traveling alone. Wrap all your gear in plastic bags for extra protection from water. You don't want all your clothes and vital gear to get soaking wet or you'll be in real trouble. You also don't want to get swept down the river completely, and you certainly don't want to try to swim to safety with a big backpack stuck to your body, so unsnap your hip belt and chest strap. If you fall or get taken under, you'll need to get that pack off as quickly and easily as possible. You should also use a walking stick if you can find one, a rope, or whatever else you can find to use as a safety net—and for Pete's sake, don't cross big rapids, or wade upstream from a waterfall. Let

CHAPTER 15: NATURE'S HAZARDS · 93

Hollywood stunt men try this, or rely on trick photography and digital effects—don't actually do it.

ATTACK OF THE FURRY CREATURES

Yes, it's true, people have been killed by wild animals. Grizzly bears, buffalo, mountain lions, black bears, and even deer have maimed and killed our kind. Most of those attacks could have been prevented, too, I'm willing to bet. For instance, the photographer who died in Yellowstone—the last photo on his roll of a grizzly bear and her cub from point-blank range: I'd say he could have taken a little extra precaution in that circumstance.

But beware. Animal attacks are quite frequent and something to really get concerned about. If I had a nickel for every small child I've passed on the trail with his throat torn out, or a dime for every time I've seen a pack of ravenous wolves take down a fully grown man like he was an innocent little lamb, I'd be a rich man. It seems almost every hike I go on I see blood scattered on the trail or bleached human skeletons with teeth marks covering the empty ribcage. Yes, I'd be awfully careful. Always bring a high-powered automatic weapon with you, and keep it loaded and cocked with your finger on the trigger at all times—and shoot to kill. Especially if you see wolves. They'll make quick work of your tender flesh. It's true. Didn't you read that Red Riding Hood story?

If you're terrified at this point and actually considered what I have just said to be true, then you have nothing to worry about. If you fear dangerous animals and respect their ability to harm you, you'll be fine. It's the people that get too close with cameras, hunters butchering warm bloody elk carcasses in grizzly country, and other risk-takers that get attacked most often. Other types of attacks do occur, albeit ridiculously rarely, in more-populated areas that border wild-animal habitat. Joggers, small children on busy trails, and campers in busy national park campgrounds are the most susceptible. Other than that, take a few precautions if the area you are planning on traveling to has a history of problems—such as Yellowstone, Banff, and some areas in Alaska where grizzlies are so common you have to push them out of the way to make it up the trail. And don't just sweat the big carnivores. Deer, elk, moose, and buffalo will not hesitate to trample you and kick your face in if you get too close—or if you try to feed them. Like me, they are deathly afraid of most American food. By the way, wolves don't attack people, despite what was said in all the books your mom read to you as a kid.

If for any reason you do have an encounter with a large animal that looks unhappy to see you, back away slowly, with no quick movements, no eye contact, no aggressive or frightened body language. It's important to look unthreatening to animals. If they feel that you aren't compromising their safety and not encroaching upon their territory, then they probably will leave you alone. There is a small chance that a big bear or mountain lion will view you as a potential meal. Again, this kind of thing is incredibly rare, but if it does happen it's important not to look like a frightened rabbit or something. If you take off running, it will make it harder for their animal instincts to resist chasing you. Besides, the animals they usually eat run from them. If you take off running they might just assume that you were meant to be chased. Don't give them any ideas. Just back away slowly, finger on the trigger of your AK-47 of course.

Don't forget about snakes either. Snake venom can be very potent, and it can surely kill a healthy adult, but it is much more difficult to get bit by a snake than you think. It's not in a snake's best interest to waste precious energy and venom on a fully grown human being. They are obviously not going to eat you. Injecting you with a little of their poison is a last resort. Their first reaction is usually to warn you with a noisy rattling tail, or else they just get the hell out of your way. Carrying a snakebite kit is a good idea if you are planning on going through highly infested rattlesnake country, but the best way to protect yourself is to concentrate on what's in front of you, pay attention, and don't let your feet step on a snake trying to take a nap. You'll stay much safer doing that than running around with your head in the clouds thinking that your snakebite kit will solve whatever problems you run into.

The living organisms you should really fear are much smaller than grizzlies and mountain lions. So let's talk about those instead of dwelling on the ones that are so glamorous, fierce, and scary. If you want to be scared of a living creature be afraid of Salmonella, E. coli, Giardia, ticks, mosquitoes, poison oak/ivy, poisonous plants and mushrooms, and rodents. Hell, you've probably got a better chance of having a tree fall on your tent during the night and smashing your body than being killed by a bear.

There's West Nile virus, malaria, dengue fever, Lyme disease, Borrelia relapsing fever, and Rocky Mountain spotted fever. You can get E. coli and Giardia from drinking stream water. The list goes on.

The best way to avoid most of the common pathogens of North America is to filter all drinking water. Also, make sure you are filtering water from the cleanest-looking water source. This will increase your chances of drinking potable water that's free of nasty viruses, bacteria, and parasites. Some water filters are better than others and it's not completely impossible for a filter to not work properly. Also be careful, especially when hiking in a nonwilderness or BLM area, that the water source you are pumping from is free of heavy metals and other soluble compounds that could be bad for your health. Irrigation water can be full of not only nasty microorganisms from cattle but also dangerous amounts of nitrogen compounds, phosphorous, etc. If any water source is questionable, try to avoid drinking it and find out more about it through guidebooks and by asking local land offices. The best rule of thumb is to find water that you'd feel comfortable drinking without filtration, and then filter it anyway.

Hanta virus is a nasty disease that is still very rare. The disease is air-borne, and can be contracted by breathing air in an enclosed environment where mouse droppings and urine have been. If you run across a musty old cabin somewhere along the trail, don't barge in to see what's in there. Hanta virus can be fought easily, but the symptoms are flu-like, and many people don't realize they've contracted the disease until it's too late. It's also possible to get infected from opening up a bear-proof food box like you would find in a campground or national park. It might even be possible to open up your backpack or food bag and, if it has been attacked by mice, and get infected. The best way to prevent this disease is proper food storage out of the reach of mice—a bear-proof box is not always proper food storage despite what a park ranger might tell you—it keeps bears out, but I don't know if the perfect solution has been found.

Okay, I'm done with my little rant. My point is simply not to dwell on horrifying encounters with large predatory animals. They're statistically a teeny-tiny threat to our safety. But let's continue to talk about food storage. One of the best ways to protect yourself is through proper food storage. Proper storage protects your food, you, and the animals. In many national parks and other popular areas with bear problems, food boxes are provided. These do a fantastic job at keeping bears out, but again, they often don't keep mice out. I've had my food ravaged by rodents in a bear-proof box more than once.

The best possible way to store your food is to hang it from a branch at least 6 feet from the trunk, 6 feet from the limb it's suspended on, and 10 feet from the ground. This is best done by tying a rope to a rock and hucking the rope over a sturdy branch at least 20 feet from the ground. Then you split your food and other stinky items (toothpaste, deodorant, sunscreen, etc.) into two bags of equal weight. Tie one bag to one side of the rope and hoist it up. Then tie the other bag onto the other side of the rope, making a loop on the top of the bag so you can get it down later. Make sure no excess rope is left dangling. Bears are pretty smart and will grab the rope and pull your food right down. Then push the other bag up with a long stick. As one bag goes up the other comes down. They should balance out above your head, at least 10 feet from the ground. When you want to retrieve it the next morning, simply hook a stick inside of the loop, and pull the food bag down. Got all that?

Yes, it's simple and complicated at the same time. There are many factors that have to be perfect in order for you to pull that off. First of all, you need the perfect tree. In most backpacking areas you'll be surrounded by somewhat scraggly conifers that can barely support themselves, much less your food. Hanging your food would be like trying to hang a 25-pound Christmas ornament. The branch sags, and if the food doesn't slide off completely it rests right against the trunk, within easy reach of a good-climbing black bear. You need to have a fairly good arm and decent aim. You must find a good-sized rock. You must find a long stick to push your food bag up in the air and retrieve it the next morning.

For some campsites, it's easy, but for others it's impossible. The age-old technique just isn't reliable. It's good to practice the skill of food hanging, but when traveling in an area that truly has bear problems, bring a bear-proof bag or bear canister. They are slightly costly food containers that are heavy and take up space in your pack, but using them is really the only reasonable way to make sure that you aren't adding to those bear problems. These aren't just sold at every 7 Eleven. You'll probably have to search online or borrow one from a ranger district or national park backcountry office. Many parks rent them, and some even require that you use them.

Although I still think that your chances of getting attacked are about a million to one, proper food storage is important. It protects you, decreases the chances of everyone getting attacked in the long run, and most importantly, it protects the bears. They don't need to be eating the crap we eat. If they do they'll get caught and shot. Once a bear learns how to exploit campers' food, they'll be a lifelong nuisance. Many times, the feds will have to bring it down. Remember: "A fed bear is a dead bear!"

The final tips I have about bear safety are to make noise. Bears aren't interested in meeting you. They would much rather hide and let your foul-smelling flesh pass by, oblivious to their presence. Near rivers this is really important. Rivers drown out sound and will make a surprise bear encounter more likely. And surprise bear encounters are probably the worst kind to have. Bears, who would normally run away from you, can panic and respond more aggressively, especially grizzlies, who tend to have less fear of humans than their black cousins. Even bear spray or a gun will rarely protect you if you stumble right into a bear that doesn't know you're coming. Also be more cautious in high winds, or when you are walking into the wind. If the bear can't smell you, it will be less likely to discover that you are on your way towards it.

That's all for animal safety, but remember once and for all: you are safe out there. Bear attacks, bacteria, mosquitoes, etc. are all minor risks that you face. Follow the necessary precautions and you'll be fine. There's no guarantee that nothing bad will happen, but there's no guarantee that you won't get in a car accident, fall down your stairs, or get shot in your home either. Don't let fear of any of these things keep you from going. Respect them, be conscious of the danger, but never dwell on it. There is simply too much fun to be had to let your microscopic chances of doom stand in your way.

CHAPTER 16

LOST AND FOUND

Getting lost, in most places, isn't that big of a deal. Usually you'll run into someone who knows where you are and where you need to go in order to reach your destination. Signs and landmarks that you'll be somewhat familiar with are also common. In addition, only a handful of wilderness areas in the lower 48 are big enough to truly get lost in for days. Getting lost is more of a problem for day-hikers anyway, who are unprepared to spend a night out in the cold, who don't have any food or water, no tent or sleeping bag, possibly not a raincoat, a lighter, or really anything that comes in handy when you're out on your own, battling the harsh forces of mother nature.

With a backpack full of gear, getting lost isn't nearly as much of an issue. You have plenty of food to last you for a long time, a warm, dry tent and sleeping bag, a water filter, and lots of warm protective clothing. If you're prepared, being lost can sometimes even be desirable for true adventurers. The point of this chapter is to teach you how to navigate in the backcountry, because it can save your life if you know how to do it, and it can kill you if you don't. That's a bit drastic, I know, but I think everyone who travels in the wilderness should know how to use a map and compass, not only for their protection, but also to enhance their backpacking experiences. Maps help you see where you're going, where the good camping spots might be, how far to water, how far you are from the top of the hill, and countless other tidbits of useful information. Carrying a topo map of the area and a compass is essential, so here's an introduction on how to use one—getting comfortable with navigating will depend on how much you practice.

USING A COMPASS

If you are completely unfamiliar with compasses, you at least know that the N points north, and when the needle is pointing toward the N, north is straight ahead. Unfortunately, I'm about to destroy the only piece of information you thought you had grasped. The needle on the compass—the stick that spins around inside the circle—doesn't point to true north. It points to *magnetic* north, which in most places is very close to actual north, but it does differ to varying degrees. Okay, I'll try not to lose you here. The North Pole is true north. When you want to head north, you want to head straight toward that North Pole. Magnetic north is a magnetic field that constantly changes, but that magnetic field is our friend—it's the driver behind the wheel of your compass; it controls that red needle.

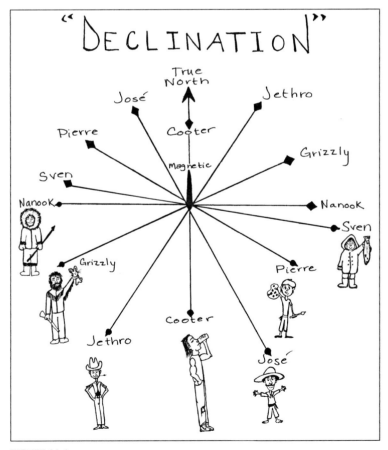

FIGURE 16.1

Magnetic north is just below the North Pole, so there is a line on the Earth where the two are perfectly aligned and your compass's needle actually points to true north. However, if you are not in line with the perfectly aligned North Pole and magnetic north, then magnetic north and true north are two slightly different directions.

To make more sense of this, look at the beautifully drawn diagram of two poles representing true north and magnetic north (Figure 16.1). Each of our colorful characters has a compass and is heading where the red needle points on each of their compasses. Notice that each person's trajectory sends them through magnetic north because each compass points to magnetic north; however, only one, Cooter, makes it to true north. Cooter, who is from Georgia, makes it to true north because for him, magnetic and true were aligned from the beginning. The others weren't so fortunate. After continuing on their original trajectory, they are all lost.

Jethro, who started in San Antonio, has ended up to the east, and as you travel further north our characters miss the mark by even greater angles. Those farther to the east and west also miss by a greater margin. Nanook of Alaska is totally dumbfounded when he realizes that the needle on his compass was pointing almost directly east instead of north. The same goes for the gentlemen on the other side. Sven of Finland has ended up in Alaska, Pierre of France is way off the mark, and Jose of Cuba is too, but he's closer because his point of origin is so far south. What I mean by that is that if you picture someone directly above Jose and draw a dotted line, the line would be farther off—draw a guy below Jose and he ends up even closer. This is exactly how magnetic north makes a compass adjustment necessary in order to go in the direction you want to travel. Don't worry, the adjustment is easy.

On most maps, the angle that you must adjust for will be indicated (see Figure 16.2). This is called "declination." I hate to use big mysterious words like that because it prevents you from figuring out what I'm saying, but I want you to know what *declination* is when you read it on the map. Most maps will give a number for declination, which represents an angle of difference, and say whether or not it is eastern declination (like what Grizzly experienced) or western declination (like Pierre experienced). Each area will have its own, and to make matters worse, magnetic north is always changing positions—you have to continually keep up to date on what the area's current declination is. It's a bummer, I know, but you'll get used to it, and it won't be a big deal anymore.

Making the adjustment on a compass should be easy. Not all compasses are the same, but most decent backpacking compasses have either rotating faces, or a tiny screw in the bottom for setting declination. It works like this: On the outside of the circular compass there should be numbers 0–360. Inside of that

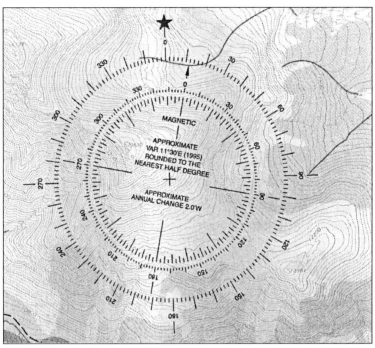

FIGURE 16.2

wheel of numbers there should be some lines and hopefully a red arrow that is painted on the compass (not the arrow that moves). This painted-on stationary arrow is for lining things up. To find magnetic north, point the painted arrow towards the top of the compass. Then get the red needle inside the arrow. Voila, you've found magnetic north. Now you just need to adjust for declination. If you have, say, 10 degrees of eastern declination as indicated by your map, then turn the painted red arrow 10 degrees to the east (to your right). Now, once you've lined up the needle with the painted arrow you've found true north. True north will now be, if all the red stuff is aligned, towards the top of the compass, which should have a stationary white mark outside of the number wheel. Notice that true north is to the west (to the left) of magnetic north. Now look back to Jethro. As you can see, true north is a little to the left of magnetic north if he is facing it. With this new information, Jethro can now find the North Pole. We just gave Jethro an "edu-muh-cay-shun" (education) on compasses. Yee-hah!

Okay, so that was some ridiculously complicated-sounding stuff. Stay with me though, and use your own common sense instead of trying to decipher what I just said if you are lost. You'll get it.

USING A MAP

The hard part is over, so don't reach for the Advil yet, your headache should subside. If you get the part on how to find true north, and feel somewhat confident about it, then the rest is easy money. It's more or less common sense from this point on, but there are a lot of things to learn about maps, especially topo maps like the ones we'll be using, which are different from your standard road atlas—but not as different as you might think. Instead of looking for a web of roads to travel on, you're looking for a web of trails—which are also roads, but for very slow vehicles with two legs. Instead of using towns as landmarks, you'll now be using peaks, streams, lakes, and trail intersections, among other things. In fact, there are so many landmarks that with a little practice, navigation will be easier than you thought—but of course, getting lost will be easier than you thought too, because a little confidence in your abilities will sometimes have you making the wrong assumptions.

CONTOUR LINES

Before we discuss different pieces of topographic maps that I've chosen, let's discuss the very important contour line. These are the lines that show elevation on a topographic map. At first they look like a jumbled mess that makes your head hurt, but they do make some sense if you give them a chance. When you buy a map and take it home, look at the contour interval, which should be printed near the distance scale. On most *Trails Illustrated* and USGS quadrangle maps, the contour interval is 40 feet. That means that each line represents a 40-foot change in elevation. Also, every fifth contour line is thicker, representing a 200-foot elevation change (5 x 40 = 200). This helps you keep track of elevation without having to count each little line. So, if the trail you plan on taking crosses 11 thick lines and 3 thin ones, all going uphill, then plan on sweating heavily because you'll be climbing 2,320 feet.

The hardest question to answer when you first start out with topo maps is how to tell whether or not elevation is increasing or decreasing. The good news is that each of the thick contour lines is labeled with a number, which is feet of elevation on most maps (as opposed to meters). This is the easiest way to tell. If at first you don't see the elevation of the line you're on, follow the line around until you run into the place where it's labeled. You can also figure it out by looking at elevation labels of lines above and below the line you're unsure of.

Okay, let's get started with the discussion of the maps I have found. Basically, we'll look at each map together and talk about the things that it is telling us. You should, by the end, get used to recognizing certain things that will come in handy for trip planning, navigation, and getting un-lost.

Let's start with Map 16.1. Ahhh, take a look at that beauty. It makes your head hurt and your eyes blurry just looking at all those damn lines. What do they mean? How the hell would that terrain really look? How do those lines translate into mountains, peaks, valleys, and ridges?

First of all, find the areas with the densest concentration of contour lines. They look the most confusing and the most intimidating. This translates perfectly to real life. Each one of those little lines stacked almost on top of each other in the center of the map represents a 40-foot elevation change. The terrain in most of this map is incredibly steep, practically cliffs in the middle. There are no trails passing through here, no lakes, nothing—just massive jumbles of barren rock, you know, the kind of stuff you get out there to see.

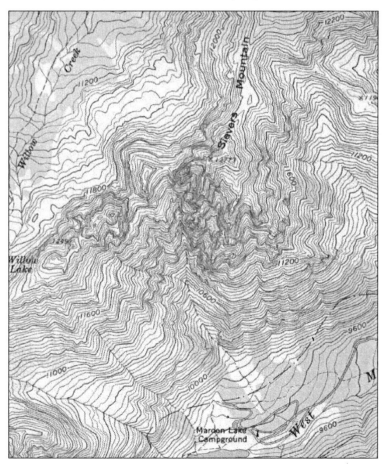

MAP 16.1

Now let's talk about those lines. Why are they shaped like that? They are all curvy, squiggly, and psychedelic man. Whoa. First of all, let's think about what an object you know would look like graphed out on a topo map. How about a thousand foot, perfectly shaped parking cone. This cone is sitting in a giant parking lot in Texas. It is perfectly flat all around it. Since the area surrounding the cone is flat, there would be no lines, just a white blank piece of paper with the cone diagrammed in the center. The cone would appear as a set of rings, each getting smaller and smaller until reaching the center—like a ringed target. Why? Tie string, which represents the contour lines on a map, around the cone. Wrap each one all the way around—one every 40 feet. The top is much more narrow in circumference than the bottom, and requires a very small ring. Finally, after 25 rings (1000/40 = 25), you've made it to the top, where your last ring is only the size of a rubber band. That's all a topo map is trying to do. Each line represents a piece of string. It shows you that the height above sea level is 40 feet higher or lower than the line next to it.

Now look at Map 16.2. This is a slightly more diverse map, but it is still covered with burly rugged terrain. On the bottom, however, we have something new—lakes. First of all, let's point out the obvious. There are no lines

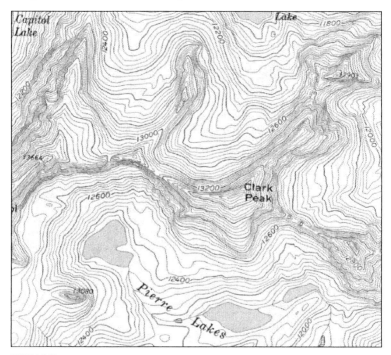

MAP 16.2

inside the lake because lakes are flat—there is no elevation change. Next, take a look at some of the other rings on the map. These circles all represent high and low points in the terrain. The lakes aren't very different. They are just low points filled with water. The part of the map where the lines are most dense (along high ridges) the circles most definitely represent peaks, not dips. Look carefully to see a few tiny circles along the ridge to the east and west of "Clark Peak."

Also take a finger or a pencil point, and follow some of the thicker black contour lines until you can't follow them anymore. Most seem to wiggle around aimlessly, but they are actually just parts to a big wavy circle. Take a second to follow the 13,200-foot line just west of "Clark Peak." See how it connects back to itself? The other lines on the map are doing the same, only they are larger because the middle of the mountain is fatter than the top—just like that joyous parking cone.

Once again, let's talk about how all the squiggling relates to a real life landscape. Envision for one last painful time the parking cone. If you mentally morph the cone into a mountain, all kinds of bumps and canyons, valleys, ridges, cliffs, and benches emerge. Your perfectly circular contour lines go from a nice neat set of rings to a chaotic mess not unlike the pile of spilled spaghetti on Daniel Larusso after he sees Johnny kissing his woman. That bastard! But, the beauty is that they're all still connected circles – just severely deformed. Wowzers that's amazing! Anyways, let's move on before I completely bludgeon this concept to death.

Time for Map 16.3. Take a look. We actually have a trail running through this one. We're getting somewhere now. There are two trails actually, marked by the faint dotted lines. Let's focus on the trail that runs from top to bottom, not the one that runs off to the east by the word "Hell." Is the trail that travels north-south a steep one? At first glance, it looks steep because the terrain surrounding it is pretty rugged. Don't put too much focus on that though. How many lines does the trail actually cross? Are many of the lines that it crosses jammed together or spread out? Finding the beginning and ending elevation is a good way to tell what you're up against. Where the two trails intersect, what is the elevation? It's about 8,200 feet, right? Keep in mind that the elevation change between two thin lines is 40 feet. Every 5th line is darker, which is just a shortcut allowing you to count 200 feet at a time. Now, find the elevation of the trail at the bottom right corner. The trail is between the 8,320-foot line and the 8,360-foot line. That's not much elevation gain overall, especially spread out gradually over this three-mile section of trail.

What are the white streaks running down the mountain from the west? Those are avalanche chutes. Most topographic maps use shading to signify areas of tree cover. This entire map is in a forest, and the white streaks are

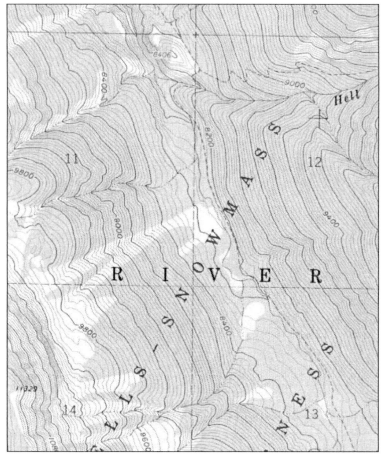

MAP 16.3

simply areas without trees. This allows you to recognize things like meadows, avalanche chutes, and the treeline.

Finally, I laughed at how this map was cut off. Notice the other trail—the one running east-west. It follows a creek canyon called "Hell Roaring Creek," but on this map all you can see is "Hell." How steep is that trail? That's right my little amigos. It is "Hell" indeed. In fact, this trail continues to conquer the dense stack of contour lines all the way up and over 12,000 feet. This trail isn't merely hell, it's a full blown biatch!

What about Map 16.4? We have a nice looking trail working its way across the southwest part of the map. This is actually the same trail that we looked at earlier in Map 16.3, but it's a different section. Notice that it's still cruising up the valley from north to south, and that the valley is starting to open up. In other words, there is more flat ground. This entire section of trail is a popular place to set up camp. Notice the white splotches along the trail. These are large open meadows. Mountain meadows can be stunningly beautiful, and these meadows, which I've hiked through a jillion times, certainly fit into that category. The area is ideal for camping. You have water nearby (which on a color map is easy to tell by the blue line running alongside the word "Avalanche"), tree cover (indicated by the gray shading), and beautiful meadows that open up panoramic views. The lines in the valley are far apart, suggesting that flat ground is plentiful. It is also a good place to go if you're not fully acclimated to high altitude—the elevation, as you can see, is between 8,500 and 8,800 feet.

Also notice all of the "V's" along the steep hillsides east of the trail. Where the lines make a V-shape there is a very faint line that looks like it's stretching

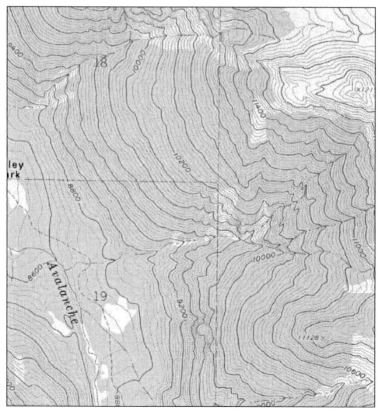

MAP 16.4

the lines, pulling them upward. All of these V's are small creek canyons. Why does it make that shape? Basically, a canyon or valley is a place where the terrain dips down as you go across it—some places more drastically than others. If you wanted to walk across a valley without losing any elevation, you would have to walk in a V shape. You couldn't walk straight across it or you would go down and then up the other side, failing on your mission to stay at the same elevation. I chose to discuss these because it is a great exercise in figuring out how the contour lines relate to real terrain. Use this line of thinking to translate other bends, curves, dips, peaks, and cliffs that you'll come across.

MAP 16.5

Map 16.5—I think this one will be it for your lesson on maps. Let's use this map to recognize as much as we can, however useful or useless it may be. What do you see? A few small ponds in the southwest corner, a couple of trails, steep creek drainages in the north, gentler canyons in the middle, the word "Wilderness" in all caps, several small circles, treeless meadow along most of the trails.

Where's the best place to camp along the trail on the northern end? What makes the spot you chose the best place to camp? Is there tree cover? Is there flat ground? Is there water nearby? Do you have to wander too far from the trail to get to camp? Tons of good spots are in the area, right?

In this area, where is the treeline (where trees stop growing completely due to high elevation)? Again, tree cover is indicated by the gray shading—green on most color maps. Notice that the 11,400-foot line separates tree-covered areas from the barren white parts quite well, except for a few spots where trees grow up to 11,600 feet.

Does the section of trail running alongside the word "Hasley" follow a high ridge, traverse a steep hillside, or pass through the bottom of a valley? If you look carefully you can see it's in a valley. For the most part, the contour lines are higher on both sides.

Finally, where is the highest point on this map? It's hard to say for sure, but it's probably in the upper right corner. What is the elevation there? It looks like nearly 13,000 feet. Can you know that's true with absolute certainty with what you can see up in that corner? Not really, huh. Because there are no labeled contour lines in that corner, it is possible that there is a ridge, and that the terrain is actually headed downhill in that corner. Based on the "V" shapes in that corner though, it probably does keep heading uphill. Go hike up there and find out you freakin' animal!

GPS (GLOBAL POSITIONING SYSTEM)

At first I hated these things. I appreciated the technology and what the tool could be used for, but still, I was reserved. It makes sense. I'm not big on gadgets in the backcountry. I'm not big on gadgets at all. I don't own a camera, a tv, or even one of them cell phone things. But then I got a GPS as a gift and things changed. Drastically. GPS is an absolutely incredible invention. Its usefulness is infinite. No one needs a GPS to survive. Humans have lived and explored without them since the beginning of time, but I'm in love with mine.

A GPS tells you, to almost an exact degree, where you are. Depending on the features of the GPS, it can translate your speed, average speed, distance to destination, time of arrival at destination, exact time, elevation, distance from your car, etc. You can also download maps onto a GPS, and then you can determine where you are in relation to the surrounding geography (as if plotting your latitude and longitude wasn't enough already). Thus, a GPS is a great survival tool when you are lost. Need to find your way back to the car? All you have to do is mark the location of your car at the trailhead, and later, when you need to get back, simply lock on to that location and the GPS will guide you there.

They aren't foolproof. You still need a map, and you definitely need compass skills, but once you've mastered orienteering, a GPS is a sensational weapon. It works incredibly well for cross-country travel, allowing you to hike without a trail to guide you, with pinpoint accuracy. All in all, a GPS can broaden your ability to get into unexplored territory while making backpacking a safer activity. You always, as long as the GPS has full batteries and is functional, know precisely where you are. Try one out sometime; they are very easy to use, but as I mentioned earlier, know how to use a map and compass frontwards and backwards before you attempt to rely on a GPS to navigate.

NO COMPASS? NO PROBLEM

Finally, before we end this painful map discussion, let's talk one more time about compasses. Please bring one with you whenever you go out. Even if it's just for a day hike, and even if you have a GPS. Batteries run out, GPSs may malfunction, you may break it, lose it, who knows. Less can go wrong with your compass, and it's good to have a backup.

Finding your way around without a compass is much more difficult and much less accurate, and although I should assume that this last paragraph will inspire you to never leave home without it, I'm going to briefly discuss finding north, south, east, and west without a compass in case you get yourself in a real mess and your compass is lost, at home, or broken.

The sun is always your best indicator of direction. It rises in the east and sets in the west. This is a dead giveaway on which direction you're heading. In the middle of the day, though, you may have some doubts. If time is running out and you can't wait till sunset to find out which way is west, you can figure it out by using a watch, or even pretending you have a watch. Point the hour hand at the sun. Halfway between there and noon is south if you're in the Northern Hemisphere above 23.5 degrees latitude. Boom, done, end of story, thank you very much! Seriously, this trick does work if you don't need precision. It will give you a general idea every time.

If you still can't figure it out, look at slopes around you. One mountainside is covered with sage, the other side is covered with a thick, shady conifer forest. Maybe there are even a few patches of snow in there. That means that the sage faces the south, and the conifer forest faces the north. Try to pick up on some of these things as you walk around. It's really quite simple, which is why I got so pissed at Anthony Hopkins and Alec Baldwin in the movie *The Edge*.

They bothered to make some ghetto leaf compass with a paper clip. Then they would scan the mountain terrain and one side of a peak would be covered with snow, the other completely barren. Hmmm, I wonder which way is north you morons? Supposedly they were in Alaska (even though they were in Canada), where at high noon the sun is right there, directly south of every tree, every bear, and other less intelligent two-legged life forms.

Yes, it's easy, but please don't throw your compass away. It's the most precise way if you really need to pinpoint your location or your route, and you will if you get out there enough. And of course you will because this book is so breathtakingly inspirational. This chapter in particular really helped put all of your fears into perspective. Now you know that you're quite safe out there.

PART VI
ECO-FRIENDLY BACKPACKING

I felt a familiar pressure building up in the lower regions of my gastrointestinal circuitry.

"No, it's something else. I must be hungry," I told myself in denial. I kept walking, my yellow Labrador trailing behind me—probably hungry too. The hill seemed to be getting steeper, my legs felt heavier and heavier. I admitted to myself that it wasn't hunger after all, and I needed to find a place to go, quick. The hill flattened out into a nice meadow surrounded by aspen trees. Not the best cover, but it would have to do. It was now or now. The others in the group were trailing behind. It was a perfect opportunity to slip into the trees and get some relief.

Nervousness crept over me as I stepped off the trail, embarking on a mission that was unfamiliar to me—to go where many men had gone before, but where I hadn't, and I didn't know what to expect. Naturally, I feared the worst. Nugget was right on my heels. She had no idea what she was getting herself into. "Stay Nugget, stay! It's for your own good, stay!" She did as I said reluctantly, like I was abandoning her, saving her for the bears to eventually attack and devour after she had lost all her strength from foraging for food, unsuccessfully, for weeks in the wilderness. She stared, painstakingly, as I disappeared amongst the ghostly white trunks of the aspen grove.

One slow step at a time I got deeper and deeper into the woods, a Ziploc bag with toilet paper and plastic shovel at my side. Finally I looked back. I couldn't see the trail, Nugget, or any of the guys, who were probably getting close to the top of the hill by now. It was me and the trees. Go time. Nervously, with a feeling of dread in my stomach, I analyzed the feeling in my intestines one more time to see if I could possibly get out of the terrible deed I was about to do. Nope. I really had to go, and time was running out.

I pulled out the green plastic shovel and started to pick at the dirt. The ground was full of roots and hard as a rock. My plastic shovel was no match for it, and the digging was slow and relatively unsuccessful. Finally, I had broken the surface by a few inches and decided that it was in the hole, or in my pants. The hole was clearly my best option. Tossing my shorts around my ankles I squatted down, unsure of how my hole-to-hole alignment was. My main concern was getting my underwear and shorts out of the way before it was too late. I struggled and nearly fell over. Should I take a knee? The squatting thing didn't feel like it would actually work. Finally, the magical muscles of my digestive system sent the goods into their final resting place—or so I thought.

It felt like a mess that could never be cleaned up had just been created. The feeling was similar to having a friend vomit on your carpet, where for one split second you wish you could move somewhere else and not have to ever take care of it. Then, a squatty yellow Labrador came trotting through the aspens. "Nugget No! No! Go away, go on git!" It was no use. She circled around behind me. What was she doing? I tried to turn around without tripping over my underwear or stepping in my pile. Before I could say "shit-eating-dog," Nugget had done the unthinkable. Shaken, I pulled up my shorts and buried a huge pile of toilet paper—the first outdoor bowel movement now behind me.

Gradually, I got used to the idea of relieving myself in such a way. Eventually, I didn't even think about it, I just did it—no differently than I do at home. Well, differently, but I did it in the same nonchalant manner. Eventually, I also was able to look at Nugget, pet her, and play fetch with her without thinking about what she had done. Ahhh, outdoor poopin'. It ain't so bad, and it makes for a hilarious memory, although I would recommend keeping it a little more private than I am. It's more information than most people need to know.

CHAPTER 17

GOOD HABITS

CHOOSING A CAMPSITE

Where you choose to set up your tent is very important to minimum-impact camping. Basically, there are three general types of campsites you can camp in. The first is an area with no vegetation whatsoever. Either the site has been used hundreds of times and the soil is barren of vegetation, or it is nothing but a big slab of rock. In either case, this is one of the acceptable places to set up your tent. You're not going to hinder the campsite's chance of recovery because as far as you can tell, there really is no chance of recovery—maybe the site is a popular designated site along a crowded trail and gets used 50 times a year. The other acceptable place to set up your tent is in a site that looks like it's never been camped in before. Unless you're planning on spending a week there, you're not going to destroy the vegetation. You'll flatten it a little bit, but it will recover just fine.

The third type of site is one where the vegetation seems to be more worn than the rest of the vegetation surrounding it. It isn't barren, but it isn't lush. In other words, you can tell that several people have chosen it in the past. You should never camp in a site like this. The site is obviously not used that much, but with repeated use it could become barren, its soil might get washed away by a few heavy rains, and vegetation may never grow back. I've seen this happen thousands of times while doing campsite inventories as a wilderness ranger. A destination that gets an average of maybe two tents per night during the summer may have up to a hundred campsites that are well worn with little hope of recovery. Do your part by making sure this doesn't happen. Camp in an area that has either no chance of recovery or no chance at becoming barren. It's the sites that are in transition that you want to avoid. The site may or may not recover, but the less worn it looks the less enticing it will be for the next camper who stumbles along.

If you are into campfires, make sure you camp at a site with a fire ring instead of building your own. In general, if you move more than a couple of rocks, you are doing something wrong. The old cliché is "a good campsite is found, not made," but the cliché is true. The wilderness is not the place to go for building rock fireplaces or digging up rocks to make a nice smooth surface to sleep on. If you do something like this you run the risk of burning eternally in the flaming pits of Greenpeace hell. On the other hand, you might want to scatter fire rings and ashes in partially worn sites, concealing the spot with some grass and twigs. If it's not obvious that it is a campsite, then the average Joe Hiker will pass by without even noticing it and pick the nice worn-out site by the lake, complete with log seats and bonfire-sized fire ring. This just helps to insure that the impact inflicted upon the area stays at a minimum and that not-so-obvious campsites have a chance to disappear.

KITCHEN CLEANUP

Washing dishes isn't exactly the fun part about backpacking, but it is important that you do it with a conscience. There are some tricks that keep you from having any impact on your campsite, which in some of the most crowded wilderness spots is truly essential.

Next time you go to the store, buy a couple of "scrubbies," dedicated for backpacking trips only. The best are the rough-textured, pot-and-pan ones, whatever you prefer. You will be scrubbing mostly pots that aren't nonstick if you eat like I do. If you like to bring separate bowls, teacups, etc., you might want to bring along a small sponge to get them nice and soaped up. Whatever your preference, it is important to dedicate a few scrubbies to your backpacking stash so you don't have to grab a moist, scummy one off the sink as you rush out the door. It also keeps you from forgetting to bring one, so you don't have to use any of nature's plant life, a dirty T-shirt, or heaven forbid, your fingernails, to scrape gunk off of dirty dishes.

Step 2 is to buy some cheesecloth. Cheesecloth is material that works as a sieve to catch particles as you're washing dishes. Although it is somewhat frivolous in an area that doesn't get much use, it is absolutely necessary in areas of high use. Unfortunately, there are too many places in the country where all rules of "Leave No Trace" must carefully be obeyed in order to keep from turning them into disaster areas. The most harmful effect of pouring all kinds of food particles on the ground is the effect it has on the area's rodents. "Feed them, and they will come." There will always be friendly mice and ground squirrels around to torment your food supply on occasion, but don't help to take rodent infestation to a new level. It's like feeding bears but worse. I've never seen anyone get attacked by a bear, but I have backpacked with someone who got attacked by a mouse. Right, Fontaine? You should have seen this crazy mouse. It broke the skin!

Use the cheesecloth to strain out water whenever there might be a few food particles floating around. If you cook pasta and drain out the water, you might want to use it. When you're scrubbing your pot later, use it again, each time emptying the particles caught in the cheesecloth into your garbage bag. When all the pots and pans are clean, get as many particles out of the cloth as possible, give it a good rinse, wring it out, and hang it up to dry. It dries quickly, doesn't take up much space, and weighs nothing in your pack. I know it might still seem trivial to go through this procedure, but go buy some cheesecloth and see if you can force yourself into starting a good habit.

Also be sure to buy biodegradable soap. Your bar of Ivory in the shower or your Palmolive by the sink won't cut it with "Leave No Trace" standards. But, just because it's biodegradable doesn't mean it is harmless. It isn't meant to go directly into water sources. Don't just rinse out your soapy pot with water and dump it into the creek. Dump it on the ground, preferably over a spot without much vegetation. Campsuds and Dr. Bronner's soaps are the most popular. Dr. Bronner's works better as an all-around soap for body, hair, and dishes.

Lastly, I would highly recommend buying a five-gallon solar shower bag, especially if you tend to camp in the same spot for multiple nights when you go backpacking. You might feel like a real city slicker buying it, but it can really cut down on the damage you do to your poor campsite. When you camp, it is almost always by a water source, and you find yourself walking back and forth along the same path, over and over again, while you're camped at that site. You carry your dishes over there, you wash your hands before dinner, you fill up your water bottles. In the morning you head down there to wash your hands after pinching one off, or just to soak up some morning sun. The person or persons that you're with do the same. Before you leave you have made a new trail to the creek from the campsite or helped to keep a social trail that was already there from recovering.

What I do is roll up my solar shower in my pack when I head out the door. When I need to filter water, usually right when I get there, I take the bag with me and fill it up. It's usually my one and only trip to the creek from the campsite, and I even bother to take a different route back to the campsite to keep from doing any permanent damage to the vegetation. If you're in an area that's relatively free of bear problems, you can hang your bag in your campsite; otherwise, pick a spot a little farther away. I wash my dishes using water directly from the bag, far away from the fragile, moist banks of the creek. I wash my hands there, and sometimes even do what the bag was intended to do, take a nice warm shower. I've even been known to filter a little water directly from the bag early in the morning before the sun heats it up. Solar showers are an unnecessary convenience just to take showers with, but they can really be used as a tool for minimum impact, and I think any serious backpacker should put down 20 bucks for one.

DOIN' THE DEW

When nature calls and you feel the urge to urinate, choose wisely. I've heard it all on the best spot to pee, and I'm not sure I believe any of them. The first rule I ever heard was to pee away from any kind of vegetation. If you squirt a little dew on a pretty flower, that flower might just keel over and die. Instead of doing this, you should go on a nice barren area or even directly in a lake or stream. At least that's what I heard, but it just doesn't sound right. Peeing in water? That sounds like the worst thing to do, but the theory behind this is that a large source of water will thin out the toxic substance, and it will become the most benign by doing it this way. I haven't been able to launch urine into a crisp clean stream yet. I stick to trying to find a place that is naturally lacking vegetation—like on top of rocks or near tree trunks.

DOIN' THE DOO

Doin' the doo for the first time is a rather unpleasant experience. I certainly dreaded it and dreaded it. Like anything, you get more and more used to it, and it gets easier. This may sound totally nuts, but by now I'd rather take a dump outside than on a toilet—especially a public toilet. Hey, you say I'm crazy, but have fun squatting on a toilet seat where thousands of other people's asses and piss dribbles have been. I'd rather be doing it the sanitary way out in the open. Anyway, the best way to do it is by burying your goods six to eight inches deep in a hole that you dig with a spade. This insures that it's deep enough to keep animals out of it and to keep a heavy rain from flooding it out of there. You don't want it any deeper than that, though, or it has a chance of getting into the nice fresh groundwater, and nobody wants that. And for Christ's sake, take your grumpers at least a couple of hundred feet from trails and any water source—hopefully even farther than that if possible.

As far as your toilet paper, it's fine to put it in the hole too. Both will decompose and become rich healthy soil in a few years at the most. Some people recommend burning the toilet paper, but if you're in an uncrowded area it just doesn't matter all that much. Some people also use the local vegetation to wipe. That's what I used to use if I forgot the t.p., but don't make a regular habit of it. It sounds great to commune with nature and everything, but please don't rip apart vegetation to make your ass happy. Also think about the billions of Asian people who don't use toilet paper at all. A few splashes of water and back to business as usual. This would probably be the best backcountry technique. Try it sometime, you oversanitized American.

Most bowel movements outdoors will be pretty simple, but there are a few situations you want to look out for. For example, many places are ridiculously crowded, and 30 or 40 people or more may be camping in a relatively small area every night for months at a time. Believe it or not, the ground can become absolutely saturated with little poopholes. Although packing out your feces may sound unreasonable, you might want to consider it if you plan on visiting an extremely popular spot. Me, I just consider another place to backpack. Maybe you should too.

Also, if you are with a very large group, say eight people or more, you might want to consider doing a group poop—especially if you are staying at one campsite for more than one evening. Dig a rectangle-shaped hole in the ground that can be straddled without having to pull off any Cirque du Soleil maneuvers. Then use this as a kitty-litter–type contraption. Poop and cover it up with some dirt. The next person comes and does the same. Odors will be much milder than you expect, and impact will be held to one square foot. And please remember to all take different paths to and fro to keep a bathroom trail from getting worn into the untouched forest floor.

PUMPING WATER

Another habit to form is how and where to pump your water. Stream banks are one of the most fragile places in the outdoors. They erode easily if used too much, so it is important to make sure that the soil surrounding the stream has a nice bed of vegetation to keep its soil in place. Unfortunately, there are popular places to get water, wash dishes, and sit, just like there are popular places to camp. Streams and lakes always have their little damaged spots along banks and shores. Take the same attitude towards these spots as you would a campsite. Let the borderline places recover and stick to undamaged areas or spots that are so damaged there is no hope of recovery.

You have to get water somehow unless you carry it all in. It's important not only to choose a good place to pump water, but to choose the best way to walk to it from the trail or from your campsite. When you walk to the stream to pump water, try not to walk on a path unless a well-worn path already exists. Once again, it's like the "picking a place to set up your tent" idea. You don't want to ruin the vegetation's chances of growing back. If the trail is wide and well-worn, then stay on it to make sure another trail does not develop, resulting in twice the damage. If you are in an area with no signs of extra trails to and from the nearest water source, then take a different route going to the water source and back each time. Trampling vegetation once won't cause any permanent damage, but if you and your group of three other people keep going back and forth to the trail or to the creek from the campsite, a path will quickly emerge. Spread yourselves out.

When staying in a campsite, use your head. Your goal is to keep from permanently changing the land. You want to leave as little evidence that you were there as possible—that's the whole idea behind "Leave No Trace." Just following these few steps would make a huge difference if every backpacker practiced them.

HELPING OUT

Now you know what not to do to keep from causing more damage. Now let's talk about the things you *can* do to actively participate in cleaning things up. I mentioned a little bit about it earlier, but I'm going to mention it again because I can, dammit.

CAMPSITE MAINTENANCE

If you find a campsite that is partially worn and looks like it would have a good chance of recovering, then stop and do what you can to "naturalize" it. That means, make it not look like a campsite so that passersby don't see it and get any camping ideas. If there is a fire ring, chuck those rocks far from the site and scatter the ashes—picking out little pieces of glass and aluminum and packing them out. Then cover up the black ring on the ground with some pine needles, dead grass, dirt, etc. Make it look like it was never a fire ring. You run the risk of someone coming along and building a new fire ring, of course, and that will have to be your call. If grass is growing on the site and you had trouble even being able to tell it was a previous campsite in the first place, then it's probably safe to tear down the fire ring. If it's a prime spot right by a gorgeous lake in a crowded area, then leave it alone—even if it's an illegal site (usually it's illegal in wilderness areas to camp within 100 feet of water or trail)—because someone is going to use it and odds are, if they are camping in an illegal site, they'll have no remorse about building a new gigantic fire ring.

Another trick I like to do with fire rings is to make them smaller. This prevents the Billy-Bob Giant Bonfire Effect (BBGBE), which happens when a slow-witted person sees a large fire ring and tries to completely fill it with flammable items. The smaller the ring, the less wood that can be torched and lost forever—eventually resulting in live limbs torn from trees once all the deadwood within 100 square feet has been used. Some rednecks will still alter the size of the ring later, which there's nothing you can do about, but you can try to stop them from getting any ideas. Remember, "rednecks with ideas, especially ones regarding fire, can cause great disaster, and they are the source of most human-caused forest fires in this country today"—*Washington Post.*

Finally, and I promise to stop obsessing over the fire ring thing after this paragraph, is to remove ashes from a full fire ring. If the fire ring is in a good place and there's no need to break it down, please do try to shovel out some of the ashes. When heavily used rock fireplaces fill up, the most reasonable option in the minds of the stupid is to build another fire ring right next to the full one. Yes, it's true: I've seen sites that looked like ancient Anasazi ruins. Three rings is the most I've seen, but I'm sure four and five exist somewhere. I hope to never see those sites, but if I do, I won't be able to resist the urge to do some housekeeping—hopefully I've inspired you to react the same way.

Other campsite maintenance duties are more obvious. If you see trash lying around, pick it up and take it home with you, but be careful. I've seen it all and I don't wish for you to see some of the things I have—shit-covered paper towels lying in a fire ring for example. Also, if you come across any kind of permanent structure in wilderness—perhaps something that was illegally constructed by an outfitter such as a log table, tepee frame, or something like that, then tear it down. Have fun doing it too, because when the outfitters return they will be quite unhappy. It's like pulling a prank on someone doing something illegal and disrespectful. Sounds fun, right? It is.

Another thing to think about are the subliminal factors that guide the decision in the average backpacker's mind about where to camp. It's really not a life-and-death decision—it's usually guided by what looks flat, what looks like a campsite, and what has a nice view. You can play a bigger role in someone else's decision than you think. If you see a campsite that is just developing or is illegal—right next to the trail or near a river bank, it is possible to make sure that no one ever camps there again. That's right. You can choose the future of any campsite depending on how much time you spend concealing it and making it look like a horrible place to camp. The ideal thing to do is to remove all traces of campers—burnt logs, log seats, fire rings, and so on. Then make it look unattractive. Throw some large rocks all over the surface, cover the site with long dead trees, branches, and other things that would be a big pain in the ass to move. The ultimate technique, although it is impractical for you to be doing with your free time, is to actually bury large pointed rocks in the ground with just the cone-shaped points sticking up in the air. Do this and no human will ever attempt to sleep there. It's been done, and it works.

Finally, there are several social trails going in every direction from most busy campsites. This causes a lot of damage to vegetation when you multiply it by a zillion campsites in the United States. Block some of the trails that look unnecessary, saving one obvious route to use. This can be done with rocks, fallen trees, or branches. Just don't cover every single trail or new ones will form.

GET 'EM MUDDY

Seeing a sign that said "Get 'em Muddy" for the first time was a great relief. It was a sign suggesting that people walk through the muddy spots on the trail instead of around. The "em" in the sign refers to your boots. Get those boots wet and muddy. That's what they were made for and why you spent so much money on them. It's fun too, tromping right through brown goo. How often do you get to do that? In many places I've backpacked, getting your feet wet and muddy is impossible not to do. So why bother going around—walk straight through that giant puddle across the trail.

So how does getting your boots muddy help out? Next time you see a muddy spot on a trail you'll realize immediately why not going around is important. Going around the mud tears up the terrain around the trail severely. Not only does it look like crap, but when there are thousands of miles of trails and millions of muddy spots, we're talking about vegetation loss that can be measured in square miles. With vegetation loss comes erosion, more trail damage, and poorer water in the closest stream. When I worked for the Forest Service, we obsessed over little muddy spots and other barriers that caused people to take a different path. You should too.

Now that you're familiar with the reason to keep trails narrow and in good condition, you can help. As you might imagine, it's not just mud and puddles that cause the trail to widen. Trees lying across the trail are a big problem—people trample right through untouched vegetation to get around them, and not just the big ones, but very small ones too. Another thing that causes problems is tree branches. It sounds silly, but some overgrown brush or low-hanging tree branches can cause damage. People avoid them just like they would a big pit of mud, and the result is the same.

I don't expect you to carry an ax to solve these problems, but try to do what you can. If you see a low tree branch and the trail widens way out around it, break it off. The tree will be fine—you're just doing a little pruning. I know it seems ironic that you are breaking off branches to help the local vegetation, but it really does work, and the little guys growing near the ground are important too, more important than I think we can truly comprehend. Anyway, this is an easy way to lend a helping hand.

Fallen trees cause big problems, and I don't expect you to lift them with superhuman strength. Sometimes the biggest problem is the limbs that are still attached. If you can, get in there and clear all the limbs off the trunk—without injuring yourself in those shorts and gloveless hands. A barren tree trunk is easy to hurdle, but one covered with branches can be nearly impossible to get through with a big load on your back. It's even tougher for horses, whose metal shoes ravage fresh grasses, shrubs, and flowers when they have to take detours.

You can do simple trail maintenance too. You don't have to bring a big shovel with you; just use your boot if you can. If you come across a puddle or tiny creek in the trail you can drain the water or help make a diversion. If you see a puddle and the ground it's on is perfectly level, there is really nothing you can do to drain it, but if one side is clearly lower than the other, you can help. With the heel of your boot, clear a nice ditch for the water to flow out downhill. You may not be able to dig deep enough to completely drain a large puddle, but you'll help to shrink it, and the water inside will evaporate faster, leaving less mud for people and horses to want to walk around.

The last type of trail maintenance you can do, which is hands-down the most important on most trails, is blocking off areas where more than one trail has emerged. For one reason or another, many trails split off and two, three, and sometimes four trails run side by side. It's silly, and does more damage and exposes more soil than most backcountry bad habits. The problem is that even a conscientious hiker doesn't know which trail is the right one to take to minimize damage. Fortunately, it's easy to tell people which one is the right one by blocking others off. It sounds impossible, but it's really easy. You don't have to cover every inch of trail with a dead tree for the subconscious decisionmaking part of people's minds to wander where you want them to wander. Establish the main trail from the beginning by blocking others off with branches and dead logs that are small enough for you to carry. If you think another confusing part comes up, then try it again. If there are no trees try to find rocks. Just laying one long stick, one inch in diameter lengthwise on a trail, can change a hiker's mind. A little can do a lot. You, by yourself, can do a lot. So feel free to pitch in when you can.

In addition to what I've mentioned, familiarize yourself with the latest official "Leave No Trace" suggestions. These should be easy to find at any information center, some trailheads, and even on some maps. Certain areas often have specific rules and tips, and you must obey them as carefully as you can. Other than that, use your head and be courteous. The less an area is altered by humans, the more attractive it will be. We're all in this together, and owe it to each other to perform many of these common courtesies. Clean up after yourself, and others if you have time, or stay at home.

PART VII

OTHER GOOD THINGS TO KNOW

THE TREK

It was the 22nd day of the trek.

My stomach problems had finally subsided. My body was transforming into an efficient hiking machine. There were hardly any pains in my body. My lungs were clear and free of the cumbersome asthma that tormented them back home. I was fully open to the experience, which was getting better by the minute as we journeyed deeper and deeper into the heart of the world's highest peaks.

Waterfalls launched off the cliffs as we continued our endless uphill battle through some of Nepal's most remote villages. The water cascaded down the cliffs, dropping at least a thousand feet before fading into a fine mist near the valley floor. High above the falls stood an immense peak. Sets of entirely different ecosystems stair-stepped their way up the mountain—thick forest, dry barren tundra, and finally thick glaciers on top, which could barely be seen through the thin clouds circling above. The narrow trail crept along the opposite side of the valley in large waves of ups and downs, passing over remnants of several large landslides.

Ahead of us was an elderly man, at least 70 years old. He carried an old backpack and a gigantic knife that dangled from his belt to his knees. Quickly he scurried up and down the hills as if the terrain were flat as a board, keeping a smooth and steady pace. I more or less choked on his dust as I tried to keep up. By the time I reached him—a solid hour later—he had stopped and courteously stepped aside to let me pass. He offered me a warm, nearly toothless grin, and talked to me in a Tibetan language. I smiled and shook my head. He laughed but kept at it, testing me with a number of phrases. After each, I only smiled back, and he gave a hearty giggle every time. We understood one another on a different level, and that was clearly all that mattered at the moment. After he ran out of questions and comments, I gave him one last smile and a polite nod of my head before anxiously moving onward—always desperate to see what was around the next corner.

After a few short miles I reached the small, barren, windy high-mountain village of Kambachen. It's a Tibetan yak-herding community at the northern end of Kanchenjunga Conservation Area Project (K-CAP), one of Nepal's several nature preserves. Roy and I sat and ate our lunch: rice, red beans, and potatoes—fresh Himalayan ones that have more flavor than a truckful of Idaho russets. The wind was howling in our ears, and very cold, having just swept across glaciers in the mountains above.

Kambachen was a funny place. There was a small wooden shower constructed near a tiny stream. It looked tattered, barely standing, like it might fall over at any moment. One of the villagers had decided to capitalize on the recent influx of tourists in the area since they opened up K-CAP to trekkers. A small sign dangled on the top of the shower. It had letters from my alphabet written on it, proof that they were trying to communicate something to me. The sign read "Hawt Chawrs [hot showers]," a good attempt in a spelling bee, but not necessarily correct. The little things are funny by the fourth week, I guess.

After our lunches were down our throats, the guides rose to their feet to lead Roy and I to the campsite du jour. We battled with the wind to set up all the tents. Behind us, clouds were covering Jannu, a monstrous, angry, vertical slab of rock that stands 26,000 feet above sea level. We had seen Jannu a couple of weeks earlier from the south side, a giant throne in the distance. Now its north face loomed behind, teasing us while we wondered just how much was covered by the clouds. How big could Jannu be?

The sun dipped behind the massive surrounding peaks while the breeze continued, forcing me to hop in my tent and do some reading. As usual, after a long day of hiking up and down in the hot sun, reading quickly turned to sleeping. By the time I woke up tea was ready, the others in our group had arrived, and the cozy giant tent had been put up for extra warmth and shelter during dinner. A few stars were making their way into the dark blue sky. I looked to see if the clouds had cleared over our 26,000-foot neighbors. Not quite, but more of Jannu was revealed. I stared and waited. The clouds were much thinner and higher up on the peak. There could be a break in them any minute. Roy came out of his tent and stood next to me, his camera tucked under his arm.

And the clouds cleared. The sky was still a dark shade of blue, a little daylight still clinging to the horizon. Neither of us said a word, we just looked, our heads tilted back to look at the giant mountains in the sky. We stood at 12,500 feet, only five horizontal miles from Jannu, which towered nearly 14,000 feet above us from our vantage point. Jannu is unbelievably immense. Other mountains on Earth aren't even in the same ballpark. The top 10,000 feet on the north side is a vertical slab of unclimbable, unconquerable rock. It's similar to El Capitan, only five times as big and sitting on top of an already huge mountain. The mountain itself has a presence without parallel. Its might weighed down on us as if we were under the ocean. All we could do was stare, soaking up the moment, trying to comprehend a tiny fragment of what we were seeing.

At that moment I felt fully tuned into my emotions, my body, and living a nomadic way of life. My feet no longer hurt, the ground felt like a mattress when I slept at night, the unhealthy diet I enjoyed at home was but a memory, going to the bathroom without a toilet was no different, air-conditioning was a splash of cool water, heat was an extra layer, television was a weak substitute for what I was getting to see, the river was my shower, my feet were my transportation device. My whole world had changed, and the purity of it all charged me with a passion to live and explore even further—to drift as far away as I could into this new, exciting dimension.

Since that trip I have slowly fallen back into my old ways, but the experience will always be a part of me. The lifestyle I lived for a little over a month pulls at me every day, begging me to return. It's been four years now since I was living that life—the simple life, the healthy life. Long backpacking trips change everything. They are nothing like a weekend getaway. You are forced to live it, not just do it for a couple of days and hurry back to burgers, television, and Pert Plus. It will make you stronger, wiser, and more at peace with yourself, others around you, and the planet we all live on.

With backpack and boots, anyone can have the most incredible journey of his or her life. On my trip I met what will be a lifetime friend, opened my eyes to the other cultures of the world, cleared my mind and body of all the impurities I have known since birth, and became a stronger, kinder, simpler, more tolerant, more spiritual, and more intelligent person. If you have the time and money to do this kind of thing, do it before it's too late. If you don't have the time and money, make it happen. It's difficult, I know. I've been trying to return to that lifestyle unsuccessfully for four years now, but it can be done. Keep trying. You'll never regret the time, money, and effort you put in.

CHAPTER 18

BACKPACKING ABROAD

So, as you've probably discovered, I took a backpacking trip to Nepal. It was a great experience. I did it with a group of students, and actually received academic credit for hiking around. It was hands-down the greatest thing I've ever done in my life, not just because I was out backpacking, but also because I was traveling outside North America for the first time.

If you are a sane person, then trekking in a foreign country should sound appealing to you, but there are some tricky things about getting good information. If you are a timid traveler, then go with an organized group. Become a Sierra Club member if you aren't already, and do one of their foreign adventures. The Sierra Club leads and organizes backpacking trips all over the world for short and medium-length service and recreation trips. They are also pretty reasonably priced since they aren't trying to make millions off of it. There are several other service, volunteer, and educational organizations that do outdoor adventures too. The back of *Backpacker* magazine is also a good source for finding organized foreign trips geared specifically toward backpacking. They have several pages of classified ads—mostly from ecotourism companies.

If you are feeling a little more adventurous, want to pay less money, and want to do things in a smaller, less organized group, then hit the books and the Internet. Again, the most common information you'll find will be outdoor adventure companies running ads and trying to get you onto their web page, but good information is out there. Personally, I think going to a local library, a large bookstore, or an outdoor store that carries books is your best bet. You can go and look at the books and get an idea of which countries have something special to offer. Nepal, Tibet, Bhutan, China, Mongolia, Russia, New Zealand, Switzerland, Ecuador, Chile, and several African countries are some good mountainous places that you might consider. There are also treks and hiking areas in rainforest areas such as Brazil, Peru, Belize, Thailand, Costa Rica, and Africa. That's what I like about looking at a selection of books at a bookstore. You get tons of ideas instantly, and you'll realize that your options are almost endless.

Trekking in foreign countries can be very intimidating. There are so many concerns that run through your head. "Is it a safe place? Is there a lot of theft there? Are there reliable maps to keep me from getting lost? Are the commuter planes safe? Am I going to get thrown in some Third World jail by a corrupt police force? Are there good hospitals? Are there deadly diseases?" Most concerns are blown out of proportion and fit into the paranoia category, but some of these concerns are real, and should be taken very seriously. Once again, if you are really worried, go with a group sponsored by an environmental agency or adventure travel company. They're a safer alternative than going by yourself or in a small group. Plus, having an expert group leader (which they probably won't be, but they might) will enrich your trip, teach you more, and allow you to find good places to go more easily.

INOCULATIONS

This is a big issue when traveling in foreign countries. I'm not a doctor, so I'm going to refer you to one. Tell your doctor what you're doing, where you're going, and see what he or she thinks. You may need to get five shots, or you may not need any. See the doctor as soon as you make solid plans to go, so that you can take the full course of inoculations before you leave. Although I'm not down with pumping my body full of toxic medicines and vaccines, I still think getting inoculated for something that's really a severe problem is a good idea, but make sure it's a legitimate threat. Vaccines are hyped up to be miracles of the medical profession, but nearly all vaccines have a long list of potential dangers and side effects. Weigh these against the dangers of the disease you're trying to protect yourself from. Odds are the chances of contracting the disease are very low, and the risk to your life is minuscule.

MALARIA

This is a nasty disease that can reoccur in bouts of a week or more for the rest of your life if you're an unlucky traveler. The current medication for it is preventative and very harsh with bad side effects. You must take the medications every day, and the best part is, they don't necessarily work. Because we humans have battled with malaria-carrying mosquitoes for decades, we have now created supermosquitoes that can handle anything. Some malaria can penetrate through a number of once-toxic substances used to kill the mosquitoes. Over the years, certain mosquitoes and the diseases they carry have developed resistance. Some are resistant to none or only a few chemicals. Others are resistant to just about anything. Your medication may work or it may not, depending on which mosquito pokes you. My favorite medication is long-sleeve clothing. If you want to, you can also cover yourself with heavy-duty deet mosquito repellent, and stay covered every second of every day while you're traveling in malaria-infested areas.

What would I do? I'd either go somewhere else, moving the malaria areas further down on my list of places to go, or I'd do nothing, take my chances, and pray to the good lord that I don't get any mosquito-borne illness—but then again, I am an idiot, so don't necessarily do what I do. Do what feels right for you. Eat well, sleep well, drink lots of water, and stay healthy in general. That will give your immune system a much better chance of kicking malaria's ass if it enters your bloodstream. If you have sickle-cell anemia (which evolved in humans living around the equator in western Africa as a natural form of resistance to malaria), run through the most mosquito-infested places on earth completely naked and send me a postcard.

PERMITS, RULES, AND REGULATIONS

Another thing to find out about before traveling to a foreign country is whether or not you need a permit to backpack, and if so, how much it costs. When I went to Nepal, for example, I needed an $80 trekking permit with a spare photo of myself to attach to it. I knew about this ahead of time and came prepared with a couple of extra passport-sized photographs of my beautiful self. Also try to find out how long the permit allows you to backpack. Perhaps backpacking is allowed for a maximum of two weeks and you wanted to spend three months out and about. This obviously wouldn't be a good surprise once you have already paid thousands of dollars for a plane ticket. The more re-search you put into this type of thing, the more prepared you will be.

Also try to find out about special rules and regulations. Every country has its own system of doing things. Regulations that you might never have dreamed of may be in place. There may be a food shortage in the villages in and around the place you're hiking in. The local or federal government may prohibit purchasing food in that area, and may require you to pack in all of your food for the entire trip. This was the case in Nepal, and porters were an absolute necessity. There's no way we could have carried enough food for ourselves and our guides for five weeks by ourselves—especially considering that most instant, low-weight, low-fuel-usage foods don't live on every super-market shelf like they do in the United States. We needed over 400 pounds of kerosene alone to support the entire crew! We even ate 100 pounds of sugar! By the time everything was put together, there were thousands of pounds of gear, food, fuel, and cooking supplies—a bit more of a load than we could have shouldered on our own.

A good way to find out about special rules and regulations is, again, on the Internet. Many countries will have trekking or outdoor recreation companies that can be easily contacted via e-mail. This is a great free way to get information, ask specific questions, and find out about the quirks of the area. Even the most up-to-date book won't be able to fully inform you. Many rules and policies change constantly and drastically almost overnight depending on the political situations in some countries. There is so much to know and discover, but the more you learn beforehand, the smoother your trip will go. Most importantly, try to focus on the rewards over the risk.

CHAPTER 19

LONG-DISTANCE TRIPS

Long-distance trips are great. A long trip will give you a vastly different experience than backpacking. Think about it. When you go backpacking you eat dried food for a few days, get dirty, wake up with sore muscles and joints. Sleeping on the hard ground, no matter how good your sleeping pad, is uncomfortable for your neck, back, and shoulders. After three or four days, you return to normal. You crave that shower, and you get it as soon as you get home. You miss ice cream and pizza and other kinds of disease-causing foods, and you make up for the shortage you'd had for those few days as soon as you get back. In other words, you rough it for a few days, and then you come home and splurge, returning to your old ways before you had a chance to forget them.

Long trips take you down another road. There are only so many days that you can dream about taking a hot shower. One day, you splash some cool water all over your body and you feel refreshed. A few days later you take a swim in a chilly lake. Pretty soon, you forget about those hot showers. Jumping in a chilly stream replaces that satisfaction with a new kind of satisfaction. You wean yourself off of burgers and fries and accept that the food you have in your backpack is all that exists—you get used to it, and you like it more and more. Instead of living in a neighborhood and occasionally escaping from your life to go backpacking, it becomes your life. Your daily routines at home transform into pumping water, folding up the tent, and stuffing your sleeping bag. Hiking, a once painful and strenuous activity, turns into something you don't even think about. One foot in front of the other you go, for hours at a time, without sore muscles, without sore feet.

DIFFERENT THINGS TO BRING

For the most part, the gear that you bring on a long trip is the same as the gear you bring on a short trip. On a long trip, however, you will of course need a few extra items, and pack a little differently than you would on a weekend outing.

First of all, you will need a hell of a lot more food, especially if you don't plan to resupply. Not only will you need more, but you will need to make sure it is particularly healthy and well-balanced. Your food bag needs to be full of calorie- and nutrient-dense food. Ramen noodles for a month won't give you the things you need. Bring a good variety of proteins and healthy fats, such as nuts, seeds, peanut butter, powdered milk, olive oil, instant beans, hummus, chili mix, and jerky. Also bring your calorie-dense things—dried fruits, candy, crackers, pasta, Cream of Wheat, cornmeal, oatmeal, rice, and other starches and grains, preferably whole grains if they are fast-cooking. To fully round off your diet, you're going to need a lot more vitamins and minerals. Dried fruits and vegetables are the best way. Leafy greens can be quickly dried at home and added to pretty much anything. Asparagus, bell peppers, and squashes are good dried as well. Garlic and shallots can be brought fresh.

To supplement your diet, it might be a good idea to pack vitamin and mineral tablets, protein powders, calorie-filled weight gainers, and whatever else you can get your hands on. If you truly did a good job of gathering protein-rich foods, a large variety and quantity of dried vegetables, and hearty amounts of whole grains and other calorie-dense items, then you'll probably do well without any kind of supplements, but it's still something you might consider.

MEDICATIONS

If you take medications regularly, bring them with you, especially if you are dependent on them. If you have asthma, bring along an inhaler even if you rarely use it at home. Many medical conditions require having an emergency supply on hand. If you are allergic to bee stings, bring what you need to combat your allergy accompanied by instructions on your backpack on how to administer it. So, if you fall unconscious, a hiker passing by will be able to figure out what is wrong with you and know how to help. The same goes for those who are diabetic or have any other unstable medical condition. I would also recommend bringing antibiotics in case you fall severely ill and your immune system fails you. Some simple over-the-counter medications—such as poison oak ointment, Advil, antacids, etc.—are also good to bring. Basically, extra days on the trail require extra precaution when it comes to illness and injury, but don't go overboard. If you are traveling alone it may be worth the money and effort to buy or rent a satellite phone. They ain't free, though, if you know what I mean.

PACKING LIGHTLY

With so much extra food, fuel, sunscreen, medication, toothpaste, toilet paper, maps, guidebooks, and whatever else you think you might need for a long trip, your load can get ridiculously heavy. Packing lightly on a long trip is far more important than packing lightly on a short one. You must be careful with every ounce. You must analyze every single thing in your backpack to see if it's possible to leave it behind. Also consider purchasing some lighter equipment—the lightest tent money can buy, a light sleeping bag, a small sleeping pad or none at all, a light backpack, etc. A pound is a big deal when you're carrying it weeks at a time, hundreds or even thousands of miles. Do you really need both of those books? Wouldn't a disposable camera be lighter? Do you really need a pound of instant coffee? See what you can do.

Also keep your clothing to a minimum. You don't need a fresh pair of socks every day. Bring two pairs of the things you wear on a daily basis: T-shirts, socks, and underwear (one to wear while the other is drying). When one gets dirty, wash it. Bring only one set of warm clothing and waterproof clothing. It may get dirty and stinky, but that's the fun part. You can be dirty and stinky and it doesn't matter. You've freed yourself from society and become just like everything else that lives outdoors—never completely clean, but just dirty enough to fit in.

RESUPPLYING

The beauty of some long-distance hiking is the ability to resupply often. It can be done easily in some areas but not in others. To do this you have to be incredibly organized. If you're out for several months and plan on resupplying yourself through the mail every week, you must pre-prepare boxes for each week. Dried, nonperishable food can go in each box, a new pair of socks or even boots on occasion, toothpaste, toilet paper, soap, fuel, maps, and other things. Remember, however, that the post office usually holds general-delivery items for a couple of weeks. Even if you can work out a deal with the post office to hold your packages longer, it is extremely important to have a friend or relative doing the mailing. You may need some emergency item, you may need more food than you had originally planned for, you may need new shoelaces, who knows. No one can perfectly anticipate what they will need and when they will need it. Friends can also slip fresh fruit or other snacks into the box for a pleasant surprise. You may also be out-hiking your boxes or vice versa. You thought 60 miles was going to be a lot of ground to cover every week, for instance, but you've been bored and could easily up your mileage to 100 miles a week if it weren't for your packages.

Resupplying is a beautiful thing, but it does take a whole lot of planning and preparation. If you are through-hiking on one of the really long trails in the United States—the Appalachian Trail, the Continental Divide Trail, or the Pacific Crest Trail—it could take days to get everything together. You could potentially resupply once a week, and if there is a town right near the trail, you might be able to buy what you need and not send yourself a box of goodies. Regardless of what you're able to do, look closely at your maps, which you will need a full collection of, and buy yourself a guidebook. This is a sure way to find out what services are available in each town (grocery, post office, telephones, etc.), and how far from the trail they are.

Every backpacker should attempt a long-distance hike at some point or another. It is such a motivating, life-changing, one-of-a-kind experience. You'll get in the best physical shape of your life, which will in turn give you energy both physically and mentally—you'll be the happiest you've ever been, guaranteed. It's really the only way to escape from everything in life—your bad habits, your laziness, your closed shallow mind. It will give you a chance to become the person you have always wanted to become. Of course, there is a slight chance that it will just completely suck and you'll hate it, but I'm trying to ignore that, okay. Just give it a shot, dammit.

CHAPTER 20

WINTER CAMPING

Backpacking in the winter is an amazing experience. I'll always prefer summertime, probably because I'm human and meant to live near the equator, but camping out in the winter can be fun too. The best piece of advice I can give you is to fully respect how cold it can get at night. Of course, in many places, a night out in the winter won't be that cold. You could be in the southern Appalachians and camp without snow and enjoy overnight temperatures in the 20s and 30s. Or you could be somewhere in the northern Rockies, shivering constantly, wishing it would just get up to 0 degrees so you could warm up a little.

The coldest night I've spent outside was during a winter in Montana, and it was a relatively balmy night. Overnight lows were in the teens, but I wasn't prepared. At the time, I had only one sleeping bag, a very worn-out bag with about a 40-degree temperature rating. It keeps me warm at 35 degrees, so I thought I would get by at another 20 degrees below that. Well, I did get by, barely, but I spent half the night doing push-ups inside my bag to get warm blood flowing through my body. Lying in a sleeping bag and getting progressively colder until you can barely move is not fun. There are several tricks to staying warm, or at least warmer.

INSULATION BETWEEN YOU AND THE GROUND

One trick is to put extra padding between you and the ground, especially if you're camping on snow or ice. Lying on ice and snow will suck the heat from your body no matter how warm your sleeping bag is. If you are pressed against it with all your weight, the cold will inevitably seep through. So, for starters, never forget your sleeping pad.

In addition to that, try to stuff extra clothes, your backpack, or whatever you can find underneath you, especially at your feet, which always get the coldest. Also wear a warm hat, and maybe even wrap your entire head in a scarf, bandanna, or T-shirt. Make sure to keep that head tucked tightly inside your bag too. If that is claustrophobic, then use a fleece jacket or something to cover your head. It will help to cover all exposed flesh and keep any cold air from slipping into your bag.

TENT

More advice—bring a tent and use it. Your little hands might freeze trying to put it up and take it down, but the 14 hours that you will inevitably spend in it will make the effort worthwhile. Remember, the sun goes down early in winter and comes up late the next day. All the more reason to set up some good shelter where you can read, play cards, or whatever without freezing your ass off. If you have access to a four-season tent meant for winter camping, bring it along. They usually have thicker walls, retain heat, and shield wind much better than three-season ones. You'll also be better off in the snow with a free-standing tent if you have one, but neither a freestanding tent nor a four-season tent is absolutely essential in most places—just nice to have.

MORE DARKNESS

Like I mentioned earlier, it is dark out two-thirds of the time or more in the wintertime, depending on how far north you are. When I go winter backpacking, I usually start at night. You can hike for several hours—and when you're moving you'll stay nice and warm. A full-moon trip is the best because snow reflects moonlight. You can see almost as well as you can during the day, but beware: if you don't know the area very well, and the trail is covered with snow and difficult to find, it might not be a good idea to travel at night.

GETTING LOST

Getting lost if there is deep snow is bad news, and good map skills and close attention to where you are become more vital. Cutting through thick forests trying to find your way back to the trail can be impossible. Hills feel ten times steeper, and there could be danger of avalanche in certain areas. Also be wary of how to get back to where you came from. A fresh dump of a foot or more snow will cover up all of those breadcrumbs you leave behind, making it impossible to find your way back unless you've paid careful attention.

AVALANCHES

Avalanches are very dangerous. Hundreds of people are killed by them every year. If you suspect that an area might be dangerous then stay away from it. It's best to hike on nice flat terrain in the trees during winter. Save the big passes and climbs for the summer. Avalanches are not something to screw around with. Always avoid fairly steep barren slopes with a lot of fresh new snow. The more loose and plentiful the snow, the more readily it will slide down the mountain—but even this rule of thumb isn't the slightest bit consistent. The only slide I've ever seen in progress was in a steep canyon in April. It hadn't snowed in weeks, there was no snow on the trail—only a little slush packed into spots along the canyon walls, and the walls were so steep you wouldn't think any snow would have a chance to accumulate. Wrong. The slush came crashing down the walls with boulders and trees and all kind of debris going down with it. When snow is subjected to strong forces of gravity, the unexpected can and will happen. Be prepared for it, and analyze the places you walk through carefully.

WATER

Another thing to think about for winter travel is the fact that water is frozen in winter—or at least much of it is. This creates a little bit of a water issue. First of all, if there is snow on the ground you're not going to die of dehydration. You can always just eat snow, but you have to eat loads of it to stay hydrated. If you want a nice refreshing bottle of liquid water for cooking and drinking—which you probably will—you might have to melt snow or ice, which takes an unbelievable amount of fuel. An unfrozen stream is a good find, but be careful. The ice on rivers has unpredictable thickness, and a sure way to get yourself into trouble while backpacking in winter is to fall into ice-cold water. Walking on ice is more life-threatening than melting snow on your stove, so think about that before you tiptoe out onto some thin ice to get a drink. Bring plenty of extra fuel.

Also beware of the limitations of your cooking stove. Some stoves, especially propane-fueled stoves, may not perform like they do in the summer. Be prepared for this by bringing extra water and a lot of food that can be eaten without cooking. Your stove may do just fine, or it may have pathetic heating power. It's not that big of a deal, but don't rely on it working perfectly, because it might not. If you are using a propane-butane mix, and the stove isn't working well, it may help to wrap fleece around it, but don't light it on fire, stupid.

SNOWSHOES

If you are planning on traveling through deep snow, snowshoes are essential. Most snowshoes sold today are too small for backpacking. Remember, you're carrying a lot of extra weight. You might weigh 150 pounds, but with a pack on you walk like a 200-pounder, and 200-pound people need bigger snowshoes than 150-pound people; so make sure your shoes are as big as possible. Big is better also because backcountry trails are often less packed than more accessible ones. The snow might be several feet deep and completely unpacked. With snowshoes the size of doors you'll still sink a little, and you need all the support you can get. Go small on the weight you carry and big on the footwear—and remember to wear sturdy waterproof boots, not just your old running shoes. Hey, I wear my old running shoes, but that is strictly a financially guided choice, and I don't go more than a couple of times during an average winter.

SHOVELS

Another fun and useful snow-season item to bring is a small shovel. Many backcountry skiers and snowboarders will have one of these small lightweight snow shovels strapped on for avalanche rescue purposes. Hopefully you won't use it for that, but you might use it to dig a fire pit, a snow cave, fort, or even a snowman. Try it, it's fun. A homemade snow cave can actually be warmer than a tent. It can be so warm that snow melts on the inside and gets you all wet. That's not a good thing, so don't get too excited about making a perfect tiny peephole of an entrance. Try it sometime.

HARSH SUNLIGHT

Another thing to think about is the reflective power of the snow during a sunny winter day. A winter trip is not the trip to forget your sunglasses or sunscreen. If you forget one or the other, you're screwed. Also remember that when you're exercising you'll be a lot warmer than you thought you'd be, especially if you're walking across an open snowy meadow in the middle of the day. With the sun out it will feel like 60 degrees out even if it's 6. One thin layer will do the trick, keeping all your other warm clothes dry and ready to go when the sun hits the horizon for a long winter night.

Other than that, most winter travel is self-explanatory. Wear warm clothes, make sure you have a very warm sleeping bag, don't walk across thin ice, etc. Stay dry, stay warm, and stay safe by at least keeping some of things I've said in mind. Winter backpacking is a lot of fun—it's much more of a challenge both physically and mentally when you're out in the cold 24 hours a day, but go the extra mile to make yourself comfortable and you'll have a great time. It is also extremely important to mention that Therm-a-Rest mattresses make incredibly good sleds. Don't be afraid to go head-first.

CHAPTER 21

DESERT BACKPACKING

The issues with hiking in the desert are essentially the same as with winter hiking—body temperature regulation, long hours of bright sunlight, and water. With the desert, things are a bit more extreme. Unless you are 100% sure, you'll need to bring all of your drinking water, and in the desert you'll need more water than you can possibly imagine. They say a gallon per day per person. A gallon is really a stretch if you're going to be on the move during the day. Bring even more than that, especially if your trip is planned for anytime between June and September. If it is planned during that time, change your plans if possible. Heat in a treeless desert is not only uncomfortable, but dangerous. Humans are great at staying cool, but the middle of the desert isn't where you want to be if you get overheated.

Other dangers are rattlesnakes and scorpions. As I mentioned before, the best way to avoid getting bit by a creature that doesn't want to bite you is to pay attention to where you step and where you stick your hands. Wear nice high boots to give your ankles a little extra protection from fangs, too, if you have some—boots that is, not fangs. A snakebite kit might be worth carrying in some places.

Wind and dust devils can create quite a disturbance. It's easy to lose the trail or your friends if you are attacked by one or the other. Try to take cover if possible, stick close to your companions, and stop where you are if you begin to lose the trail. Getting lost in the desert is a big issue because of the lack of water and the extreme summer heat. Taking an unexpected turn and getting lost for a day can easily end up with dehydration and death. I know it sounds a bit extreme, but never underestimate the importance of water. It's as essential as oxygen, and in the desert, you'll need to drink almost as often as you breathe.

Alright, now that I've made desert backpacking sound terrible, I'm going to tell you that it's not. Spring and fall temperatures can be mild. Gentle streams trickle through canyons, forming an oasis of green grass and cottonwoods. The canyon walls are so steep that you spend most of the day in the shade and hardly break a sweat. The desert, although it's harsh in August, can be a calm, quiet playground in other months. The desert provides a unique experience that cannot be found in alpine mountains or dense forests. The more of it you discover, the more appreciation you'll have for it. The canyons of the Escalante River in southern Utah are absolutely stunning. My jaw hurt by the end of my first trip there from having it dropped open all day in awe. Visually, I still think it's the most incredible place I've ever been. In spring and fall, when it's still too cold in the mountains, there's simply no better place to go. Try Death Valley National Park, Escalante National Monument, Glen Canyon National Recreation Area, Zion National Park, Bryce Canyon, Grand Canyon, Arches National Monument, Canyonlands, and dozens more throughout the desert country of Utah, Colorado, Arizona, New Mexico, and California.

CHAPTER 22

GEAR MAINTENANCE

Gear maintenance is probably too important to stuff in the back of the book like this, but I didn't want to confuse anyone in the beginning. Taking care of your equipment is really essential. I hate taking care of things—it's a problem I do have—but when I have taken care of my gear like I should, I have noticed a big difference in their cleanliness and comfort. Your tent, sleeping bag, sleeping mat, boots, water filter, and backpack all require special love and attention or they will whine and pout until they stop working altogether.

TENT

Your tent is probably the most important thing to take proper care of. If you neglect all but one piece of equipment, make sure the tent is the lucky piece of equipment that does get some attention. A tent is your rain shelter, your house, and on a rainy night it provides as much if not more warmth and protection as a sleeping bag. Tents are also the hardest piece of equipment to take care of. They are typically the most high-maintenance of all the gear you have. Rainflies leak easily and tent poles break often. A leaky rainfly isn't a big deal, but a broken tent pole is—if you don't know how to fix it.

First things first, let's talk about tent poles. Most poles have an elastic cord in the center. This allows the pole to be flexible and fold up. What also allows bending and folding is the fact that poles are segmented. In other words, every foot or so there is a space, and another tube follows, then a space, another tube, and so on until you've reached the other side. These tubes can be separated and folded at the space in between by pulling the two apart. When you pull the two apart, there is a little metal reinforcement that makes the pole firm and rigid when they are all connected. This reinforcement can be located on the outside or the inside of the tube depending on what kind of tent you have.

This reinforcement, although it is essential, is the root of all evil. Sometimes it gets stuck in the tube just a little bit. You barely notice that it looks shorter than the rest, think it's no big deal, and set up your tent as usual. As you bend that pole to fit it into the hole on the other side, you hear a snap, feel a release in pressure, and your heart sinks at the same rate your tent does, until both are lying flat on the ground, lifeless. I've been there, and the sad thing was that I didn't think it was a big deal. "Oh, the rainfly is waterproof, I'll just lay it over me and everything will be fine if it rains." It did rain, and everything was fine from a survival perspective, but I was wet, wickedly cold, and awake all night long as ice water was dumped in a fine mist all over me.

The worst-case scenario is actually having the tent pole break. At the time, I wasn't much of a repairman. My friend had some duct tape, which I thought could fix anything. Duct tape *can* fix anything except broken tent poles. The good news is that over time I did learn how to fix them, and it's really easy. What happens on a tent pole that has the reinforcement on the inside and metal tubing on the outside (most tents are made this way) is that the tubing on the outside snaps. Although it is made out of metal, it is incredibly thin to make it as light as possible. If the reinforcement on the inside gets stuck a little, there is less to support it from the inside, and the pressure put on the tubing multiplies. It will almost certainly break. It's like physics or something. I can't explain it, but I am sure it happens. I learned that from my own keen observation.

If the pole does break, remove the broken part. This can be done with a pocketknife, a Leatherman, or even a rock. Don't try to patch anything. If it's broken, it's broken, but you can make it fully functional again in a few minutes. Once you've removed the cracked part, try to file down the tube until it smoothly fits with the next segment again. Basically, you have shortened one of the segments and nothing has changed. A tent pole that is a centimeter or two shorter still works. You won't even notice a change. And don't forget to fix what caused the problem in the first place. Pull out the reinforcement that got stuck. If for any reason you have an unfixable break in your tent pole, rummage through your tent's stuff sack and try to find a repair kit. You should know what's in there ahead of time, of course, and make sure there are pole segments for making broken poles functional. The segments are usually about four or five inches long, and slide over the rest of the pole, surrounding the broken area. This will certainly fix things until you get back to civilization where handy tools that are too heavy to lug around with you are readily available.

The simpler care of your tent is important too. First of all, try not to let it sit out in the hot sun for days at a time. Your tent is made to sit in the dark and keep you warm while it's nice and cool out. The more you leave your tent in the sun, the more stress you'll put on its ability to keep you dry during a good rain. Also make sure it is always dry when you store it. If you pack it up wet and don't use it for a month, it will get covered with mold—completely covered. At that point, it's easier to throw your tent away than clean it. Even if you can get it clean, the smell will linger for the rest of its days.

Finally, if your fly leaks, which it eventually will if you keep your tent long enough and use it frequently, you may need to seal the seams. It's usually the seams that allow water to leak through. Buy a little bottle of this liquid stuff (Aqua Seal) that leaves a residual waterproof layer—kind of like rubber cement. It works on shoes and raincoats too. Try sealing the seams before trading your tent in for a new one. It may fix the problem completely and extend its life by several years.

SLEEPING BAG

This is your next most important thing to take care of. It keeps you warm if all else fails, so make sure that your sleeping bag doesn't fail too. There are really only two rules with sleeping bags—keep them completely dry and store them loosely. By loosely I mean not crammed into a small sack. This will kill the "loft" of your bag. It's this loft that keeps you so warm. By storing a bag in a compacted stuff sack for weeks or even just a few days, you will decrease your bag's temperature rating significantly. Stay on top of this and never leave your bag stuffed up in its sack for more than 24 hours. Hang it in a closet or put it in a really big cabinet. Leaving it open under your bed will work too. Keeping it dry is easier. Bring a pack cover or trash bag for extra protection during heavy rains, and don't fall in any rivers. Wrap it up in a trash bag if you are crossing a really gnarly river. Also, if you are crossing a really gnarly river, slap yourself in the face and turn around. You are making a bad decision.

SLEEPING MAT

Sleeping mats are unnecessary, but most people prefer to have them because they make things much more comfortable—and they keep you warmer too. Taking care of them is easy—don't get them wet, don't jump up and down on them, and don't use them for sledding in less than a foot of snow. The simple Ridge Rests and other mats that you don't have to blow up with air are hard to screw up; Therm-a-Rests are much easier, but still hard to poke holes in. To take proper care of a Therm-a-Rest, don't walk around on it while it's blown up. A sharp rock or stick could poke a hole in it. If you do poke a hole in it, which can be microscopic in size, you must first find where the hole is by submerging it in water if it's not immediately obvious. A tiny hole can be fixed with a drop of Aqua Seal. A larger blowout needs more work. Read the directions for fixing it carefully. Most Therm-a-Rests come with repair kits containing Aqua Seal and a few large patches for big blowouts.

BOOTS

Taking care of your boots is easy, but not always what you feel like doing when you come home from a long backpacking trip. There are too many different kinds of boots to make any generalizations here, but there are a few rules to go by. First of all, do what you can to make your boots waterproof. If you have leather boots, cover the leather with waterproof conditioner. This will protect not only the outside of the boots from deteriorating, but the inside as well, which will tear and rot away much easier if they are soaking wet. Also treat the leather parts of your boots with leather treatment, conditioners, and oils as frequently as possible, especially if your boots are leather on the inside, which is common with really expensive boots made by Raichle, Lowa, and Montrail.

Storage of your boots is important. Don't leave them wet and covered with mud, sitting out in the sun. They will turn into petrified stone that will be painful for the first few hours of your next trip. Always wash mud off of your boots as soon as possible. Let them dry gently, not like a raisin in the sun, and oil them up when they are dry to loosen them up again. It's also a good idea, if you have time, to loosen them up again by wearing them for a while. Don't be too obsessed with your boots though. They are made to be beaten up, covered with mud, soaked with water, and worn for hundreds of miles. Put them to the test, but be nice to them when they are on vacation.

WATER FILTER

Some water filters cannot be taken care of, but some can. Some stay together forever, never to be cleaned, never to be messed with. I sometimes prefer the higher-maintenance filters because I don't like picturing all the nasty stuff that has been filtered out, gathering inside a filter, festering, and rotting. Most MSR filters need a lot of care. They must be taken apart and cleaned frequently to keep the water flowing through. They filter out very small particles and start getting clogged as you send more and more water through. If you take care of them, they will last for a very long time. Clean your filter regularly if possible, and always disassemble it after a trip, allowing all the pieces to air dry to avoid that festering, rotting action from happening. If you have a filter that doesn't need to be cleaned, then please disregard this last section. You don't have to do a damn thing to take care of it other than trying to purify the cleanest water you can find.

BACKPACK

Well, you really don't have to take that great of care of your backpack, but let it dry out if it gets wet, always empty it out right away when you return so it doesn't get that funky smell, and never leave it on the floor. If I've learned anything about backpacks, it's this simple rule. Breaking or tearing a sturdy backpack is almost impossible, but crushing a buckle with your foot as you walk through the house at night is very easy. I've done it twice. I'd also recommend, if you are putting your backpack on a plane, to cover your buckles with tape, bubble wrap, or whatever else you can find that will add some protection. That's the only other way I've broken a buckle—never on the trail—but avoid stepping on buckles at camp.

ey, the book's over. That's it. Time for a cheesy ending. Well, I did it. I finished the book. It was a lot of work, you know. I need a vacation. I think I'll go see what the Wind River range is up to. See you up there!